UNBALANCED

SEARCHING FOR TRUTH
BETWEEN RELIGION & CULTURE
(and really good Mexican food)

JONATHAN TONY

ISBN-13: 978-0692731147 (Jonathan Tony)
ISBN-10: 0692731148

Unless otherwise stated, Scripture quotations are from the Holy Bible, New International Version®, NIV® Copyright © 1973, 1978, 1984, 2011 by Biblica, Inc.® Used by permission. All rights reserved worldwide.

Scripture taken from *The Message*. Copyright © 1993, 1994, 1995, 1996, 2000, 2001, 2002. Used by permission of NavPress Publishing Group.

Cover design by Steffan Clousing.

Editing by Carlene Garboden.

To Brittany.

It'd probably be pretty bad not to dedicate your first book to your wife, right? Thanks for listening to all of my thoughts while I figured this thing out and for making me do this.

Contents

"Sometimes religion gets in the way of God."

- Bono

Chapter 1

Inside Outside

Why I'm Nervous at the Circus

"Raymond is married. He has children. Good, good family. God-fearing. Church every Sunday. All of us. God-fearing people. We're scared to death."[1]

Everybody Loves Raymond

I was 16 years old and my church was putting on yet another play. Dozens of people were involved in the production. It was a big deal, and by big deal, I mean it was a massive hit with the residents of the Pearly Gates Senior Citizens Home.

If you've never been in a church play, you may be surprised at how un-churchlike some people can get behind closed curtains. It's a battle for stage time. Just imagine Broadway meets *Braveheart*, with a hint of *Toddlers and Tiaras*.

I've never considered myself an actor in any way at all, and drama kids always made me uncomfortable. (If you don't know why, then I'm betting you were a drama kid.) Still, I enjoyed participating in my church's productions, because it was a chance to be around people I liked, and I felt like I was accomplishing something for God.

Surprisingly, I liked being in them even though I never got a leading role in the cast. I was always Man #3 or Townsperson #4. If someone got sick, I would get to be Man #2 and have a few lines, but I was never important enough to have my own lapel mic. I had the roles where you had to awkwardly lean over and speak into someone else's mic hidden on their vest, so it looked like you were having an intense conversation with their neck.

This one particular night was different though. They wanted an opening act. Due to my love of *Saturday Night Live*, I'd written a comedy skit with a friend, and the church leaders asked us to open the night with it. Of course I jumped at the chance to have my own lapel mic. This was going to be my chance to have more than two lines.

More on my big acting break in a moment. First, let me give you a little backstory.

I feel like I am Benjamin Button of the church. I was born a 75-year-old uptight, conservative who knew what was right and what was wrong. I was passionate about God, the Bible, and taking over for Pat Robertson on *The 700 Club*.

Back when I was in high school, I really tried to be the kind of Christian I was supposed to be, or what my perception of a Christian should be. I wore Christian T-shirts. I prayed before I ate lunch. I carried my Bible in my backpack just in case anyone on the basketball team wanted to ask me how to spell *Habakkuk*. I tried to invite my friends to church events as often as I could. It was my counteroffer to not being invited to any of their parties.

At church events, I'd often hear these amazing stories of how some kid from the middle of Arkansas saved his entire high school by just wearing a Christian knock-off T-shirt, like *GAP: God Answers Prayers*. I'd feel guilty because I wasn't having the same success with my T-shirt evangelism.

Surprisingly, no one at school wanted to attend my church events no matter how much I asked. Not the plays. Not the youth group pizza parties. Not even the battle of the bands. What part of no alcohol, Bible memorization, and abstinence didn't sound like fun?

I couldn't comprehend what it was like not to go to church. People would say, "Yeah, I go to church." But what they really meant was, "I go twice a year." For me, I didn't just go to church—I lived there. I ate there. I got mail there.

I grew up in the Bible Belt of America. Not just the belt, but also the Bible pants and Bible shoes. I was in church nonstop, and I couldn't understand why it was so hard to get someone to come even just one time to a place I went to all the time. That must be how Sears employees feel, too.

All right, so back to my big lapel mic moment . . .

I thought this time my friends would finally come see the awesomeness that was my church. They would finally hear the Gospel presented in a totally cool and relevant way—with catchy song and dance numbers performed by middle-aged, tone-deaf white people. They would finally want to know Jesus and come to church. And they would maybe, I don't know, put me on their shoulders and carry me out of the sanctuary like Rudy.

At this point in time, I had been praying for three specific friends from school to come to my church. I hadn't been able to get them to come to a church event yet. I would mention them at prayer meetings. I wrote their names in my Bible. I really did care about them and wanted them to know Jesus like I knew him. I hoped my opening skit would be the perfect opportunity to finally get them inside the church walls.

(This was a classic church "Bait and Switch" maneuver. Just like the youth group bait and switch: "Hey, we're having a pizza party! Oh, what's this Bible doing here? I guess we should just open it and see what we end up talking about.")

The night of the play I looked through the curtains and there on the very front row I saw not just one, but all three of my friends. I thought, "This is the night! This is what I've been praying for. They will see this production and start coming to church with me."

I was excited and nervous at the same time. The same way I feel when I go to a Chinese buffet.

I went out onstage, with my very own lapel mic, and performed my skit so well, I'm pretty sure it would have brought Will Ferrell to tears. Immediately after, I rushed out to the foyer by the front doors to get a drink of water and saw all three of them heading outside. They said, "Hey, that was hilarious, Jon! We're glad we got to see you do it."

I excitedly responded, "Thanks, but wait until you see the rest of the night!"

"Oh, we have to leave, but we'll see you at school tomorrow."

I was speechless. I must have blacked out for a moment because I don't really remember what I said. I was just trying to get them to stay. I think I mumbled something and used a lot of hand gestures.

But they didn't stay. There was nothing appealing to them about sitting through a play that had cost thousands of dollars to produce. They didn't care about the lights and music. They didn't care about the prayer cards we had prepared for the end of the night. They didn't really want anything to do with my church.

What they wanted was to be my friend.

For years I stayed locked up inside the walls of my church. I liked it there, but I never knew what was really outside of it.

Many churches have a sign at the exit of their parking lot which reads, *You are now entering the mission field*. I understand the intent behind a sign like that—if you're inside the church walls, you're secure. You're here to be spiritually fed and not challenged. You're safe within these walls. But out there? That's where the lost people are. Out there is where people need God the most.

I went to a small Christian school until I was in high school. My dad was a part-time pastor. My mom was a children's church teacher and was involved with a variety of other ministry groups. My sister, Melissa, led the music in our youth group. I was inside the church all the time.

Here's a quick breakdown of my typical Sunday when I was in high school:

Time	Activity	Location
9:30 a.m.	Sunday school	At church
10:45 a.m.	Sunday morning service	At church
12:15 p.m.	Quick trip to Taco Bell for 39 cent tacos	Approximately 1 mile from the church
12:30 p.m.	Youth choir practice	At church
2:00 p.m.	Regret my Taco Bell decision, pray for mercy and healing	At church
2:30 p.m.	Possible nap or friend hang out	Preferably close to church so we could easily get back to church
5:00 p.m.	Youth leader meeting	At church
6:00 p.m.	Sunday night service	At church
7:30 p.m.	Friend hang out	Someone's house close to the church

Now here is a breakdown of the rest of the week:

Monday night

My high school's Fellowship of Christian Athletes meeting. Luckily, you didn't have to be an athlete, because I didn't have any time for sports with all of my church activities.

Tuesday night

Youth band practice, possible racquetball afterwards with church friends. Maybe play in a church league basketball game.

Wednesday night

The best and biggest night of the week—youth group. Followed by Wendy's or a movie at someone's house.

Thursday night

Lead my small group. Small groups are weekly Bible studies. Some churches call them community groups or cell groups. Calling it a cell group always freaked me out a little bit because it sounded like we were all going to be stuck in prison. Actually, "prison" would probably describe Bible study for some people, though.

Friday night

Go to the movies with friends from church. Nothing R-rated.

Saturday night

Go to the other cool youth group in town, and then
go back to my youth group for a Saturday night
prayer and worship service.

This schedule would shift throughout my high school years, but
it is no exaggeration of my teenage life.

I don't regret it, though. I don't blame my parents for sheltering
me. I don't blame any pastor or leader for pressuring me into
church. I liked church. I liked church people and doing church
activities. I liked getting to use my gifts for the Lord. I learned
how to play guitar and piano because of church. I had an outlet
to speak, perform comedy, and get into writing because of
church. I have millions of hilarious, fun, and meaningful stories
of youth choir tours, mission trips, and tons of other events.

I think I will always like church, and I'll be on the front lines to
defend it when people want to tear it down. There are
wonderful people in it who really care about their communities
and their neighbors. There are many people I know who have
given so much of their time and money to help others.

Yet, for all the good the church has to offer, I fear that it can
become its own barrier to its people. It can become shut off from
culture. It can close itself off from changes happening all around
it.

The walls we put up to block out the evil of the world become
the walls holding us inside. Walls that have us constantly
stepping away from a world Jesus stepped into.

It makes me think about Luke 10:2:

[Jesus] told them, "The harvest is plentiful, but the workers are few. Ask the Lord of the harvest, therefore, to send out workers into his harvest field.

What hits me is Jesus doesn't say, "Ask the Lord of the harvest to bring the harvest in." Instead, he specifically says to pray that workers would be sent out.

Out.

We pray the Lord will bring the harvest in—inside our walls. American churches spend millions of dollars each year to make Christmas and Easter Sunday impressive productions, not far from the amount spent on a regular Sunday morning's wow factor these days. I don't even know if I'm against all of that. Sometimes I wonder what the apostles could have done with some intelligent lighting, a smoke machine, and skinny jeans.

I'm all for good programs and catchy events. I'm for choir specials, church plays, youth retreats, and kids camps. I'm for keeping the doors of the church open in a myriad of ways. But I think if we spend most of our time praying for people to come to us, we are missing the Great Commission's command to *Go*.

I remember going to the circus when I was a kid and being amazed when the acrobats would come out and perform. Their routine was always the most stressful part of the night for me. The trapeze swinging. The tightrope walking. The acrobats stacked on top of each other juggling fiery batons. All this without the safety of a net.

A lot of this anxiety came after I watched *Batman Forever* and saw Robin's whole acrobat family, The Flying Graysons, fall from the top of the big tent and die. I was amazed, and yet, so nervous,

19

watching these tightrope walkers go back and forth on such a tiny little line of wire. From where I was sitting, the line was so thin it looked like they were walking on air. I just knew I was going to watch Robin's family plummet to their death at some point... or watch Two-Face come in and shoot-up the place.

I often feel like an acrobat myself. Minus the leotard. I'm up at the top of the big tent trying to balance on a tightrope between two sides, the church and the rest of the world.

Each side is demanding I make up my mind, but I don't want to make up my mind if my heart is in both places.

Which side do I lean more towards? Which side do I end up falling into? Is it possible to balance on this wire between the two and never choose one side to fall on?

Why do I have to choose?

Have we only been given one choice? You can either love the church and hate the world, or you can be accepted by the world, which means ignoring, or even mocking, the church.

Maybe I'm not the only one who feels like I am balancing between the two sides. Maybe you feel like an acrobat too. Maybe that means there are more than just two sides to be on.

In the pages to come, I will share my personal stories and thoughts I've gathered on my journey through both of these sides, and in between them.

Let's take an introspective look at Christian culture and the rest of the world it seems to disconnect from so easily. Why is there a divide? What is the church's perception of the world around it? What is the world's perception of the church? Can we find a way to bridge the ever expanding gap that has grown between them?

I believe we can find some peace between a church that fears the world and a world that misunderstands the church.

Singing in my dad's church in Anthony, FL. I had no choice.

Chapter 2

Don't Mess with the Formula
How the Top Two Greatest Albums Almost Never Happened

"Even in literature and art, no man who bothers about originality will ever be original: whereas if you simply try to tell the truth (without caring twopence how often it has been told before) you will, nine times out of ten, become original without ever having noticed it."[1]

C.S. Lewis

What is the church?

When we say *church*, most people have an idea of what it is to them. Most of us think of some sort of building. Maybe yours has stained glass windows all around the walls. Maybe yours has a baptismal behind the pastor's podium. Maybe yours has a massive organ no one ever uses except on Christmas Eve. Maybe yours has pews so old the cracks pinch your butt when someone down the row stands up. Maybe yours has a steeple. Maybe that steeple is being used by AT&T as a cell phone tower to make a little extra cash for the church. If it's not, it should be. It's a genius idea.

We all have different images coming to our mind when we think of church, but most of them seem to revolve around the same type of image. But what is the church?

The church is like a pointillist painting. I only know what a pointillist is because mine won second place in 7th grade at my school's art show. A pointillist is a painting or drawing made up of individual dots.[2] When viewed at a distance, all the dots combined create a picture.

So let's zoom way out and look at the church as a pointillist painting.

Looking at the whole picture, the Christian church is made up of millions of people all over the world. It's not a building.

Zoom in a little closer and we can see it's made up of different groups of people within the whole picture. Some are united by their shared beliefs about certain matters in the faith. Some are together simply because they are in the same area of town.

Zoom in a little closer and we see the church can even be defined as two or three gathered together.

To say the church is merely a group of people who meet on Sunday mornings for an hour or so is missing a few of the zoom levels. This is also why it's dangerous to generalize about its problems.

23

Most church services kind of look the same on a Sunday morning. Basically just music and preaching. Some churches meet in homes throughout the week. Some churches around the world have to meet in secret. There's no one set way that church must be church. The church is so much more than a building, a service order, offering baskets, and old people wandering aimlessly in the foyer.

There is no one-size-fits-all church. Actually, there's no such thing as one-size-fits-all in general. Whoever coined that term was way off. It should be *one size fits people in this general size*. Just because I can put the shirt over my head does not mean it fits, Walmart. Check your facts.

Some people are wired differently. Some don't connect with God through singing together at church. Some people are not audible learners, so sitting and listening to someone talk for thirty minutes or more with no visual aides makes them want to ram their heads through a pulpit. Those same people could go on a nature walk and come back in tears after connecting with God in his beautiful creation. I usually come back with poison ivy and random bite marks that make me wonder if I'm going to have to suck out the poison or slowly die.

Some people are more hands-on when it comes to learning. So if music isn't how you connect with God, and if you're not an audible learner, church can be quite a drag. To force all believers into a Sunday morning church formula is dangerous. We need to look for more ways than one to spread the Gospel and to bring others into the mix. I'll be the first to admit it's tough to come up with refreshing ways to present ancient truths. I like Sunday church, so figuring out how to do something outside of the formula I grew up with is difficult for me.

We've used the same formula for so many years, it's almost hard to come up with anything outside the box. And maybe we don't want to. I'm the type of person who gets the same thing at restaurants every time I go. I'm trying to change and be more adventurous, but it's not easy for me when I know what I like. I don't want to waste my precious ten bucks on something I'm going to want to spit out. Maybe this same mindset applies to pastors and churchgoers. We know what we've been doing, and we know what we think has worked. Why risk changing it up and getting a new result we don't like? What if the result is something unfamiliar to us?

Brian Wilson of The Beach Boys pretty much wrote all of the album *Pet Sounds* by himself. When he first pitched what he'd been working on to the rest of the band, they all hated it. His bandmate, Mike Love, told him not to screw with the formula.

They had a signature sound revolving around signature topics, like surfing, girls, cars, having fun, and driving through hamburger stands. When Wilson showed up with deeper, meaningful songs with no driving drumlines, it totally clashed with what they'd been doing all along. Eventually, he convinced them to join in on the production. And what happened with *Pet Sounds*? It's currently the number two greatest album of all time on *Rolling Stone's* "500 Greatest Albums of All Time." It even had a major influence on *Sgt. Pepper's Lonely Hearts Club Band* by

The Beatles, which sits in the number one spot. Paul McCartney has even said "God Only Knows" is his favorite song ever.

We have to be open to some *Pet Sounds* ideas and new formulas with church. We have to be open to bigger ideas about what church means. We have to see it from many different zoomed-out and zoomed-in views as we look at this massive pointillistic painting.

Remember, Jesus said, "Pray that the Lord of the harvest would send laborers out," yet we spend so much time and money trying to bring people into a building. God forbid, literally, that Sunday is the only time we have church in a week. God is clearly a God of diversity and the Kingdom comes in more ways than one. The charge Jesus gave us is to preach the Gospel and love each other. Have church as much as possible, and whether or not you need stained glass, is up to you.

I grew up in Florida and going to the beach has always been my favorite activity. It relaxes me. It entertains me. I love taking a nap under my umbrella with the sea breeze keeping me cool from the sun. Napping by the beach is my equivalent to going camping and sleeping under the stars. All I need is the sound of the waves. I think I'd always like to live as close to the beach as possible.

For some reason though, I have just never gotten into surfing. I've tried it before, and maybe one day I'll get my own board. Right now, I just Boogie Board. It's always fun to see the middle school students running past me with their surfboards while I am walking to the water at the same time holding my sweet

Boogie Board from Walgreens. I'm usually too embarrassed to make eye contact with them. What would I even say?

> "Sup, bros? Perfect A-Frames up and down the beach, huh? Yeah, I'm just gonna be over here ripping up some of this knee-deep water."

To add to my fears, I've heard stories of surfers clinging to their board for dear life after a bad wipeout in some of the rougher waters. The board is your best friend when you've lost your strength. That's what makes surfing such an intense sport. No one ever clings to their tennis racket for dear life. People don't usually drown while playing a round of golf; that would be a heck of a water hazard.

A foam board can save your life if you're drowning, but if someone hands you a surfboard in the middle of a motel shootout it's not going to be of much help. If you're falling out of a plane, a surfboard can't save you. However, I suppose riding one would at least make you look cooler as you plummet toward the ground—Flying Graysons style.

Different objects can be lifesavers in one instance, but completely useless in the next near-death experience. There is no one-size-fits-all lifesaver, and there is no one-size-fits-all church formula that will meet everyone's needs at every point in their lives.

We need diversity.

There really are only two main requirements I've noticed about a church when you get down to the core: It's all about Jesus, and you should meet together with others.[3]

On the night Jesus was arrested, he prayed in the garden for us.

> *"[I pray] that they all may be one, as you, Father, are in me, and I in you; that they also may be one in us, that the world may believe that you sent me. And the glory which you gave me I have given them, that they may be one just as we are one: I in them, and you in me; that they may be made perfect in one, and that the world may know that you have sent me, and have loved them as you have loved me."*
>
> *John 17:21-23*

Jesus desires a unified church. He didn't say the church needed stained glass and a steeple. He didn't pray that it would have at least one hymn sung each Sunday to keep the old people happy.

He prayed that we would be one.

A certain church community may not fit someone's life in the way they need it to. If it's mostly people aged 55 and up, maybe a fresh out of college 22-year-old won't fit very well in that church's demographic. There are churches with younger congregations and louder music than some senior citizens would want to be at. There are Sunday morning services I happily avoid each week. I'd rather jump out of an airplane with a surfboard than attend them.

And that's okay. We can still be one. The church is not a building; it's a movement. It's a family stretching all over the world from generation to generation.

Christians disagree about many issues, and we can waste a lot of time trying to win others over to our views. I don't think we're meant to agree on everything. There is no way millions of people can all have the same views on every subject matter. We're too diverse for that to really be a possibility. If we did, we'd be a cult instead of a community. The problem is we can be really bad at disagreeing and moving forward.

Diversity does not have to prevent unity.

My faith is a bouncing ball flying down the stairs. I'm not really sure where it's going to end up sometimes. That's not to say I have no concrete beliefs, but I've realized one of the most common themes in the Bible is people of faith saying to God, "What am I supposed to do now?"

I read the psalms of David and one of them will have something like, "Trust in the Lord at all times. He gives great gifts and always looks out for his people." And the very next psalm will say, "I'm out here in the wilderness and I think God may have forgotten me. I'm all alone and about to die. Please, Lord, kill off everyone who is trying to kill me. Seriously. Just let them have it . . . Selah."

Now either David was schizophrenic, or he was living in the real world. And all of those diverse psalms ended up in the Bible and God was cool with it. It takes a long time to pin down what you believe and why you believe it. Then, you can end up in the wilderness having your faith tested like you never expected. And with that testing, your faith may come out on the other side looking different.

The church is in a constant progression. It is always evolving. It's like we're in a perpetual puberty, never quite shaking off the awkward years. Our voice is cracking. We are trying to pass off a thin row of hair as a mustache. We're sweating a lot more.

> *And we also thank God continually because, when you received the word of God, which you heard from us, you accepted it not as a human word, but as it actually is, the word of God, which is indeed at work in you who believe.*
>
> *1 Thessalonians 2:13*

The Word of God is at work. It's an unfinished process in us while we walk the earth. We're going to get stuff wrong. We're going to change our minds. We're going to look different.

I've been in church since I was born. I had to go. Now I choose to go. I choose to join into a community of people who believe in God and want to share His love with others. I've seen church cultures change, and I've seen them hold onto an ideal so heavily that they disconnect themselves from reality.

I've been ahead of the game, and I've been way behind. I've been right about some matters, and I've been too stubborn to see where I was wrong. I've been merciful, and I've been unforgiving. I'm a mess, but I'm a hopeful mess.

Earlier in this chapter I asked what the church was. So then, what is *not the church*? Or what is *the world*? If you don't go to church, you've never hear about the world, at least not the way the church defines it. You may not know you're an outsider.

The world can be presented as the opposite of the church. The anti-church. If the church moves right, then the world moves left. If the church thinks black, the world thinks white. The church likes their all-beef burgers medium well, the world is trying to pass off quinoa burgers as edible.

The church and the world are two completely different territories. The world begins on the line where the Kingdom of God ends. To use a quote from the history books, it's like when Mufasa told Simba, "Everything the light touches is our kingdom."[4] So in the eyes of many Christians, the church is Simba's kingdom, and the world would be the elephant's graveyard.

Separating the two territories is not wrong, because there is clearly a distinction in the Bible. Jesus said, "If you belonged to the world, it would love you as its own. As it is, you do not belong to the world, but I have chosen you out of the world. That is why the world hates you."[5]

There is a difference between the church and the world. Or at least there should be.

Still, I can't help but sing, "He's got the whole world in His hands," when I hear it. Not just because it's catchy, but because I think God actually does hold the whole world. Both territories. He loves both sides just as much.

31

There should be a distinction between the church and the world, but if the church positions the world as its opponent or enemy, we'll never love like Jesus loves.

We're a diverse species. Each of us is designed uniquely, and we will have different views and different passions. The church, too, is full of its own types of people who have their own types of differences. It could easily cause chaos, but diversity does not have to prevent unity.

The only shot that the church has at making it is by remembering it is under the grace of God.

I'd have given up by now if it weren't for the grace of God. And that's what keeps me coming back to church—the grace of God. It's knowing I'm allowed to get things wrong. I'm allowed to be different than I was a few years ago. I'm supposed to evolve.

It's a process. A movement. A progression. A bouncing ball flying down the stairs. The Word of God is at work in the church, but we've still got a long way to go.

Chapter 3

Silent Monk Screams

Why Some Pain Sticks Around Longer

"Numbing the pain for a while will make it worse when you
finally feel it."[1]

Harry Potter and the Goblet of Fire

I can practically quote *Dumb & Dumber* to you, but I can't
remember what I wore yesterday.

I can tell you how tall Michael Jordan and Scottie Pippen are and
what year Kobe Bryant was drafted, but I can't tell you what my
brother-in-law does for a living.

My wife remembers every event we have coming up with
friends, but she can't remember how our thermostat works.

Despite numerous corrections, my Greek grandpa from Cyprus
called me "Johnson" for the first five years of my life.

It's funny how our memories work, isn't it? Our brains are working nonstop making sure we remember to breathe. They are miracles sitting inside of our heads. Yet, for the life of me, I can't remember what I came in the room for.

We all remember moments differently. Some moments float away never to be thought of again, and some are eternally cemented in our minds, and we are unable to ever forget them.

I can remember certain situations or big punch lines, but everyday dialogue is harder for me. Still, there are certain lines from my life I can recall quite easily. Certain quotes I wish I would have forgotten about by now. They are burned into my brain, and I can remember everything about the moment they were said like a snapshot permanently on file in my hard drive.

I'm sure you have some as well. Maybe too many. Maybe they influence your decisions to this day, subconsciously and consciously. We all have them. Why do they stick around for so long?

I miss elementary school. Not just because I miss trading snacks at lunch like it was Wall Street, it's also because I miss being the same height as my peers.

I was growing up all right for a while, but by the time puberty hit, I began to realize I may never achieve my dreams of being a professional basketball player. Not a lot of 5'6" guys dunking on LeBron. That is actually why I began playing music. Music is a glorious alternative to athleticism. Exhibit A: The Notorious B.I.G.

Actually, I remember the very first time I felt physically inferior amongst my peers.

I was in fourth grade and I was sitting on the floor outside my classroom before school talking with some friends. Conversations among fourth graders last for about ten seconds at a time. Whose dad was the strongest? What snacks could you trade from your lunch? Who was that week's guest on *Larry King Live*? You know . . . kid's stuff.

All of a sudden, a girl in my class sitting on the other side of the hallway ended her ten-second conversation and looked down at my legs. Without hesitation, in a tone of importance, and genuine cruelty she declared to me, "You have scrawny legs."

And that was it. It was all she said, and, like a hit-and-run, she moved on to the next ten-second conversation of the morning.

This was the first time anyone had ever said anything to me before about my appearance like that. It was the first time I'd heard I might not have been up to the physical standards of the average 9-year-old.

I didn't cry. I didn't get up and leave. I didn't even respond. I just absorbed it.

I remember sitting there and staring at my legs and wondering for the first time in my life if I did, in fact, have scrawny legs. I wondered, "Is this something she says to all the guys?"

It was a stupid, pointless comment from a dumb girl who I'm sure doesn't remember saying it now. I'm sure many people have heard much worse, and it should have rolled off my brain like a million other comments I can't remember now. But here I am, two decades later, and I still remember it. And it still affects me. I don't like my legs.

I've tried various kinds of leg exercises and excessive amounts of running over the years, and nothing has ever beefed them up. I don't know what it is; but I'm just not built that way, and I have never had the money for calf implants. I don't really know how they work, and I'm not sure I want to know.

I've never really been able to shake off that sentence I heard 20-something years ago. I've just grown up with it always banging on the walls of my brain. That one sentence sticks around after all this time.

Have you ever thought about the monks in monasteries high up in the mountains of Cambodia, or wherever monks go to do their "monking"? I've done a lot of research on monks. And by research, I mean using Wikipedia and watching the *Kung Fu Panda* movies.

It's amazing how they take vows of silence for years at a time. What if they stub their toe in the middle of the night? Are they allowed to project any sound of pain? I wonder if there is a silent-monk-scream they are taught.

Vows of silence sound impossible to me, but I have to say, the monks all look kind of peaceful around each other. Maybe our churches would be a lot more peaceful if no one was allowed to talk.

The problem with people going to church is that people go to church. The church is made up of ordinary people who have decided they want to congregate together. There is no extensive, military-esque training you have to go through to become a church member. No one is standing there with a cattle prod to keep everyone in line. It's just full of everyday people who do everyday actions. Like saying dumb stuff when they should have kept their mouths shut. Some people are wonderful to be around until they start talking.

I speak from experience. I've been the hearer, and I've been the speaker. I've been the wounded, and I've been the one who wounds. It's funny how the church can take on so many images and people can hold so many different perceptions of it.

For those of you who think the church is perfect, or even just better than the people on the outside of it, you are blind.

For those of you who think the church is evil and a roadblock standing in the way of progress, you need to get all your facts straight and stop generalizing.

For those of you who think that Gospel music has gone too far, Kirk Franklin has got news for you.

I bet if you stop and think, you may be able to pull up a couple of words you've heard in the church that have stuck with you longer than other words.

I don't know what it is about the wounds of the church, but they seem to stick around the longest and make a deep, dark, painful impact on our lives.

Maybe it's because we hold the church to a standard we don't hold the rest of the world to. It's like when a student sees their teacher out in public with the rest of the world, and then they realize their teacher has to shop for groceries, too.

I've known pastors over the years who didn't go to movies because of this same kind of perception. "What will people think of me? What will they think I'm here to see? It's not worth the risk or the potential mess of dealing with it."

We do this with the church, too. People think, *You're not supposed to hurt us; you're not supposed to be like us regular people.*

A common claim people tend to make about the church is that it is full of hypocrites. And they are right. It's totally full of hypocrites, but hypocrites are everywhere. The church is made up of the exact same people who make up every other group in life.

We're not silent monks in the church. People hurt people. And it sucks. I'd love to find an angle around this fact and be a little more optimistic, but I honestly can't.

If you go to church, you will be hurt at some point. There's no chance of dodging it.

There is another story from fourth grade that is still stuck in my brain.

I was at a pool party at my friend's house. Everyone had gone inside except me and my friend Brandon. We were still in the pool training for the Olympics. We'd have probably made it to the Olympics, but Brandon got a Nintendo 64 that year.

The call of pizza and ice cream soon overcame our desire to keep swimming; and we decided we'd head inside, but not until one last dive.

"Brandon, watch my dive!" I yelled like an idiot.

I ran to the back of the pool deck; but before I could get there I stepped into the drain because the cover was a little loose and I didn't see it. My scrawny leg fell in all the way down to my knee and it scraped off my skin so bad that it didn't even bleed at first. It was just white.

You grossed out yet?

It quickly started to bleed and I was in so much pain I couldn't even emit a sound. I just sat there silent-monk-screaming until Brandon noticed me. I was in immense pain and afraid all at the same time. I put my chlorine soaked hands over the wound and wondered if I'd need to be airlifted to the nearest hospital. (I had been watching too much of the show *Rescue 911*.)

Brandon raced over and helped pull me up. I limped inside with him and asked one of the forty moms at the party for a Band-Aid. And a slice of pepperoni. I got cleaned up and left with some gauze around my shin.

I remember this story so clearly, because I still have a scar on my knee. It was a long time ago, and it's not super noticeable now. But if you look closely at my right leg just below my knee, you can still see it.

I went to my friends' houses millions of times, and I remember some random activities and stories. But I don't remember those moments like I remember the story of how I got my leg scar.

Our minds have a power to distinctly remember the events that hurt us. We remember where we were, what was said, and what it felt like. Maybe even what we were wearing. Scars connect us to stories in a deep way. Deep enough to still show on your skin twenty years later.

When we have a scar story from church, it's especially painful. The church isn't supposed to hurt us; the church is supposed to heal us. It's an unholy sucker punch when you open yourself up to a place you think is supposed to ooze love, only to be left scarred.

It's hard to forget it, and it's hard to move past it.

I once asked my sister if she was planning on having kids anytime soon. She responded, "I'm not sure. I have some really great names picked out that are too good to give to a dog." And that's how we make decisions in my family.

I haven't named a child yet. I have only named my dog, Walter. I can't imagine how hard it's going to be to decide on a name once the time comes. Some great names can get ruined because of an association someone may have to the name. You probably have names you'll never give your kids, or dogs, because you knew someone at some point in your life you didn't like.

Brittany says we can never name our child Martin because there was a creepy kid named Martin she knew in elementary school who told her he had her name tattooed on his butt. So Martin is out.

We all have triggers that can bring someone to mind or take us back in an instant to a specific point in our lives. Have you ever been out somewhere and smelled something and it reminded you of a place in your past? Just the other day I was in Target and the smell of the freshly mopped floors smelled exactly like my high school. Instantly, I was transported in my mind back to Vanguard High School's cafeteria waiting in line to pay for lunch. I was embarrassed to be on reduced lunch, so I would try to hide how little I was paying for my meals from my friends.

This brain trigger is known as an olfactory memory—the linking of smells to an event, person or thing. I only know this because in 7th grade I had to write a report about our sense of smell.

Maybe there are songs you don't listen to anymore. Songs reminding us of past relationships that ended painfully, or songs we were listening to during a difficult time in our lives. I have some. I'm not hung up on past relationships; I'm married to an amazing woman. I just remember how the stories ended, and they hurt. Even though I am not still hurting from the break-ups and experiences of ages ago, I can still feel a sting when I hear the songs.

I think this same kind of situation happens when some people come near a church. It's not the same pastor who hurt them. The catty church lady who always had some comment about everyone isn't there anymore. You are too old to now attend the awkward youth group you were forced into, lonely and out of the loop. Nothing is the same anymore about the church, but just being there brings back those same feelings. It makes you not want to listen to the song again.

It is understandable to be hesitant or resistant to people or places when your trust is broken. Trust is like your credit score: it's really easy to destroy, really hard to build back up.

Whenever I meet someone new, I don't have a reason not to trust him or her, but I also do not have a reason to give that person my full trust. I can be a pretty trusting guy by nature, which explains why I've been ripped off so many times. So over the years I've become more cynical and less likely to trust someone immediately.

Trust is not a given in relationships, and it shouldn't be assumed. It can only be earned and lost.

Still, it is dangerous to attribute one person's poor track record of trustworthiness to someone else. To say, "Church A hurt me, so Church B will as well," is not fair. It's not logic you use in the other matters of your life. It can't be or you'd never get anything done.

Have you ever been in a car wreck? Millions of people have. Yet we are still on the road with strangers every day. Doctors misdiagnose and make mistakes all the time, but we still go to doctors.

I understand the tension of this logic, though; because if you've ever gotten food poisoning at a restaurant, you probably have never returned to it. (I'm looking at you, Checkers.) Certain scenarios of bad experience are easier to move past than others. And attending church may not be as necessary to your life as visiting the doctor when you're sick.

The church has become a target in the eyes of many, perhaps rightfully so in many cases. It broke your trust. It misused your time. Let's not even talk about all the scandals right now. There are terrible people who have done evil while proclaiming they love and serve Jesus. It's not hard to recall these stories from over the years.

Just turn on TV at 2 a.m. and I guarantee you there will be some "preacher" trying to sell something. I've seen Mike Murdock try to sell special breads supposedly baked in Jericho's brick ovens. They were guaranteed to heal you if you ate them. I'm not making this up. I've also seen him sell a piece of red fabric, which somehow represented the blood of Jesus, and if you stood on it or slept with it, you'd be healed. This is complete bull, and the name of Jesus gets associated with it. These people on TV are scam artists, not disciples of Christ. And because of associations like these, the trust scale for all things Christian has gone way down for many people.

Sometimes I wonder if Jesus would have been hired for any marketing jobs today, because he really seems to be bad at it. Choosing and allowing ordinary, dumb people to bear your name and take your cause to the world is not a strength you'd want to put on your résumé.

"Let's see here, Jesus, this says you've fed thousands of people with a few loaves of bread and fish. Gave sight to the blind. Wow, even brought a guy back from the dead? Impressive. A lot of community

service time, which is great. Now, let me look at your team leadership skills . . . All right, so one of your team members sold you out for thirty pieces of silver? And another one chopped off a guy's ear? And you have followers in leadership who have had affairs and embezzled money from your own churches and ministries? Yeah, sorry, I don't think you'll be a fit here for us. You aren't good at putting a team together."

It burns me to my core when I see this type of spiritual manipulation. It's not just TV preachers; it is politicians who claim to be Christians just to win votes. They use their "Christian ideals" to win votes from those who believe the future of the faith rests in the hands of legislators.

The problem with the church is it is made up of people. If we could just get rid of all the people, we would probably like it a lot more.

Dumb. Lazy. Greedy. Manipulative. Selfish. Unsympathetic. Abusive.

We are the church. These are the kinds of people we have in it. And I have been all of those attributes and continue to be them on a weekly basis. But God loves me. And He loves the other idiots, too.

I guess I still have scrawny legs; but most days in Florida, it is just too hot to wear pants. So I wear shorts. I don't really have a choice. Odds are, nobody is walking by me and stopping to think, *Wow, look at those scrawny legs.* If they look at me, they are most likely thinking, *Wow, he needs to stop cutting his own hair.* Maybe one day I will love my legs; but for now, I must live with them, and be grateful I even have them.

Adulthood has taught me that life is all about doing stuff you don't want to do. I don't want to pay my mortgage. I don't want to vacuum the house. But I have to do these things, so I do. I get over the parts I don't like, and I live life. And I can be pretty happy when I quit complaining and start looking for the good.

Maybe it's what adult church life has to be at times, too. I'm entering into a place that has hurt me and has annoyed me. I really don't want to be around it sometimes. But I have to be here. I'm choosing to be here. I am choosing to be in community with people I don't always like. It's part of maturing in my faith.

I view the church as a family. Think about your family. I mean everyone you are related to. Are there people in it who you disagree with? Are there people in it who have hurt you worse than anyone else has hurt you?

I believe most would answer yes, but not many people have changed their last names because of it. It's the same way I feel about being a Christian. Christians say and do some really dumb stuff, but they are my family.

Our families prove that the ones we love the most, and who love us the most, can hurt us the most.

As we age, I think most of us start to see our parents in ourselves. Whether it is words and phrases we swore we'd never say, mannerisms we hoped we'd never have, or simply our basic physical features. I've looked in the mirror quite a few times and seen my father. His belly is coming for me like a vengeance-seeking movie villain.

We are all a product of our families in one way or another, but we are not destined to repeat the same mistakes. History may often repeat itself, but it doesn't have to.

Who are we becoming?

The more we become like Jesus, the less we look like our pasts. Jesus is the saving grace of the church. He is the hope of becoming someone better than who we may fear we are turning into.

The scar on my knee from the pool party has healed and faded, but it still shows. I have many scars from church, too, and some of them still show.

So why am I still hanging around a bunch of selfish, arrogant, insecure hypocrites? My simplest answer is because I am a selfish, arrogant, insecure hypocrite. I fit right in. And God welcomes me.

I see a lot of bad in the church. In America, we are trained to look for the bad. It's sad that it comes so naturally to us. Our knee-jerk response is to prove ourselves worthy by proving someone else wrong. The church is full of this same nature.

But for all the bad, I still can't give up hope on what it could be, what it was made to be, and the good I see in it now. Apostle Paul described the church as a body whose head is Christ.[2] Just as Christ's physical body was wounded, so his church body is wounded and marred.

I believe one day we will see Jesus' hands and feet, and they will still bear the scars of the cross. The same scars he showed to his disciples after he rose from the grave. His scars will not remind us of our sin and shame; they will remind us of his extravagant love and the grace which brought us to him. If Jesus is not ashamed of his scars, we don't have to be ashamed of ours.

We are in need of healing every day; I don't deny that. The more the church starts to recognize this, the further we will go. The difference I see between the people of God and everyone else is this: the people of God realize we are so screwed up that our only hope for functioning is by the grace of God.

I need the church, because it is God's, and I am invited to be a part of it.

Scars and all.

Chapter 4

Hollywood Moses
Why Christian Movies are So Terrible

"If history were taught in the form of stories, it would never be forgotten."[1]

Rudyard Kipling

When I was 5 years old, the movie *Home Alone* came out in theaters, and I lost my mind over it. It was the funniest thing I'd ever seen in my short life. I was obsessed. I watched it every day when I got home from school. Many times I would just fast forward to the scenes with all the traps at the end.

When *Home Alone 2: Lost in New York* came out, I remember my family took me to see it on opening weekend. I did the same thing to *Home Alone 2* that I did to *Home Alone* and watched it until the VHS tape got eaten up by our VCR. It was also the reason I was deathly afraid of Central Park until I was about 26.

Home Alone. The Sandlot. Jurassic Park. Father of the Bride. Back to the Future. These are movies I watched in my adolescence more times than I can count. They all have kept their charm over the years. I watch them even now and still love them. These movies are well-made and well-told.

How can you not love movies? We all have favorite movies. My all-time favorite is *The Dark Knight*. (This has nothing to do with what I'm about to say, but I just wanted to get it in the book.)

There was a point in time where Christians were not going to the movies. My family loved movies too much to take part in this resistance, but I heard a lot of families from church avoided the theaters. And if you couldn't go to the movies, you were stuck watching movies at home. Worst of all, you may have been stuck at home only watching Christian movies.

There are a million Christian-made movies which go straight to video, as they probably should. Every once in a while, one will make the jump to theaters, and Christians will flock to support it. They support it, because they want more Christian movies, or because it is the alternative to bringing non-Christians to church. If we can get them to come see a movie with us, surely it will change their hearts. And for some, it has.

I remember when *The Passion of the Christ* came out while I was in high school. The controversy, surrounded by the subject matter of it, made it one of the most financially successful movies of the year. I still feel like it was the first modern Christian movie that wasn't hokey, filled with bad actors and bad cinematography. And the subtitles made it much more authentic than the Jesus we'd all seen in our church plays— white, overweight, Southern accent. Over the years, Jesus has been portrayed by a lot of white guys who can't remember their lines.

In those old movies, Jesus always looked confused. I guess they're trying to make him look holy, but to me he always comes off like, "Where am I? What am I doing here? Who are you people?" It was like his mom just left him alone in Kmart.

When *The Passion* ended, it was dead silent in the theater. No clapping. No one moving. Just sitting in the dark. You could hear the sound of sniffling and see people wiping away their tears. My friend Drew was the only person I know of who had the audacity to eat popcorn during it. I remember walking out of the theater and seeing people praying. I walked a bit closer and heard a teenager repeating the Sinner's Prayer. It clearly was, and still is, a powerful movie.

Passion made Mel Gibson the new Christian golden boy. We loved having someone so cool and well-known on our side. I mean, this was Mad Max! This was William Wallace! He was our Hollywood Moses sent to deliver us out of bad church plays and cheesiness and into the promised land of professional quality films and red carpets. We had such high hopes until he was arrested for drunk driving, went on an anti-Semitic rant, and had his face plastered all over every media outlet, along with being depicted quite frequently on *South Park*. So we had to put our beloved Mel Gibson behind us. Now he sits in the garage of our hearts with the rest of the stuff we don't want to talk about anymore. Like WWJD bracelets and TestaMINTS.

The search for our next celebrity icon continues. Tim Tebow is kind of filling in the gap while we wait.

There are many who have tried to put their hopes in Kirk Cameron. Hey, I grew up watching *Growing Pains,* and I'll always have a soft spot in my heart for Mike Seaver. I'm just not sure he's got what it takes to be our Hollywood Moses.

Box office numbers can throw you off. A movie can be the number one movie in America, and then you see it and find out it is one of the worst movies you've ever seen. It happens constantly.

It takes a lot for me to go to the theaters to see a movie these days. I have to really want to see it on the big screen. Then, I always have to make the decision of whether I want to take my wife to a movie or whether I want to send our children to college. I also like when it has a plot, but clearly America doesn't feel the same way.

Seriously, how many *Transformers* movies will they make? The answer: a billion. Some people don't care about the scripts; they just want bigger machines and bigger explosions. I like to think every room in Michael Bay's house has some sort of explosive set rigged for when he enters. Michael Bay doesn't just walk downstairs; the floor explodes, and he falls through the ceiling.

I try to trust reviews, but those are misleading, too. I can't trust critics fully because they are too harsh, and they love the artsy movies I hate. There are too many cynical and bitter critics for me to go see movies based on their reviews alone. That's why I like reading fan reviews, but they can be horribly off. I saw someone gave *Teenage Mutant Ninja Turtles* five stars, which is a crazy enough sentence as it is, but this was before it had even come out in theaters. I read the review and all it said was, "It looks like it'll be good!" Seriously?

Christian movies will really throw you if you go see one based off of fan reviews. One example is Kirk Cameron's *Saving Christmas*. Shortly after it had been released in theaters, I went and checked the movie reviews online. Amazingly enough, it had a rating of five stars, in the fan reviews section that is. Critics were not so much in the holiday spirit and tore it to shreds. It was quickly listed as (and I'm not making this up) the worst movie of all time.[2] That means *Gigli* was better. That means *Spider-Man 3* was better. That means every Adam Sandler movie was better. That means *Santa Claus Conquers the Martians* was better. That is an actual movie.

But somehow, the fan reviews gave it five stars. I can't prove this with facts, but my hunch tells me all the five-star reviews were from Christians and old people who were lost on the Internet trying to email their grandkids.

I read a few of these five-star fan reviews, and here is a list of some of them:

> *"These are the type of movies we want to see and our family needs to see. Keep bringing movies with value in the theaters."*

> *"Very good movie, tells you the real true meaning of Christmas."*

> *"It's a low budget film, and moved along pretty slow. But I support Kirk Cameron and the message he is delivering."*

> *"Kirk Cameron is a wonderful inspiration, this was a wonderful movie showing the true meaning of Christmas. We need more Christian movies and to get our world back to a more wholesome entertainment environment."*

And my personal favorite:

> *"The movie was great for all ages. Can't recommend it enough. Other than what appeared to be wine in the glasses in the last scene, I can say I would tell anyone in my church to attend. We laughed incessantly. Refreshing and theologically accurate and deep movie."*[3]

Did you notice a theme in these reviews?

Christianity creates products that only appeal to Christians. What if you went to a shoe store that only sold size 12 shoes? It would be awesome for people who wear size 12, but for the rest of us, we'd never go in there. Remember, there is no one-size-fits-all.

The Christian market tends to work in the same way. It can be a great album, but only if you're a Christian. It can be an amazing conference, but only if you're a Christian. And it's not just stuff like worship albums or church services, which would make sense to mainly appeal to Christians.

It's funny how we take anything and slap a Christian label on it and call it a Christian product. There are terrible movies that Christians would never see had it not been about Christian themes with Christian actors they are trying to support.

I spoke with a friend of mine who works as a film critic. He said, "Do you know why Christian movies are so terrible? It's because they start out with a message instead of a story. They are completely driven by the agenda of the message, and the story is just a means to fill in the gaps."

When I heard this reasoning, it made so much sense to me. Christian movies don't suffer from low budgets, bad acting, and bad script writing alone, although those factors don't help. What so many of them lack is a story. A story is what draws us in.

My favorite movies have many great scenes, but it is the story that draws me in and hits my emotional buttons. *The Dark Knight* has some incredible cinematic moments, but the themes, the struggle, the pain, the perseverance, and the hope of the story are what make me love it and watch it over and over again. (Sorry, I couldn't help it. I had to talk about it.)

Go back and read those reviews for *Saving Christmas*. Pick one out that says anything about the story. I didn't just cherry-pick reviews to list out; they were all like that. None of the reviews talk about the story; they only talk about the message. How great the message was. How important the message is. How wonderful Kirk Cameron is. Though I'll admit, I talk about how wonderful Kirk Cameron is in all of my Fandango reviews, too. Even the ones he's not in. I do it on my Yelp reviews, too. "The food here is excellent. Try the corn fritters! Kirk Cameron is a wonderful person."

The story is immeasurably important. Many mainstream movies will sacrifice the story for special effects, action scenes, or jokes, too. When I watch a movie, I want to be moved. I want the story to drive the movie. I want to see special effects, but only if it will add to the plot. Special effects with no story are a waste of time to me.

Tons of movies and TV shows will just be a series of gags without any decent plot line tying them together. This happens. Then that happens. And then this happens. Lack of story can be dangerous to any show or movie, but for Christian productions it can have a much worse result.

Here's what happens when you begin with a message instead of a story: you become a preacher on the side of the street yelling at people. You become the person telling everyone they are going to hell without any context or love.

Have you ever gotten advice from someone you didn't want advice from? It's frustrating and annoying, and if the person doesn't have a place in your life to speak advice, you are just irked and want to avoid them.

Unsolicited advice is annoying. Unsolicited condemnation is disastrous.

When you begin with a story, your message doesn't have to be so blatant; the story pushes it for you. It is also proven to be more memorable.

Why do you think Jesus told so many parables? There are forty-six recorded parables of Jesus. In fact, Jesus loved stories so much that a lot of his answers to questions were simply stories.

It would go like this: someone asks Jesus how he should define who his neighbor is. Jesus could have said, "The guy next to you is your neighbor, dummy." Instead, Jesus would answer with, "There was a man walking from Jerusalem to Jericho . . ."

The Bible contains way more stories than sermons. Stories stick. Stories burn into our brains better than facts.

Before Ray Charles passed away, he was able to see most of the filming for the biopic based on his life, *Ray*. He was able to give feedback and insight into what was really happening and what he was really doing to more accurately capture the scenes of his life they were portraying. He gave Jamie Foxx first-hand tips on how to emulate him. It's no wonder Foxx won an Oscar for his performance.

Most biopics don't have the benefit of being able to discuss their depictions with the people the biopics are about. They may have research, but they don't have the personal touch and descriptions from the person whose story they are telling. Everyone thought Daniel Day Lewis was an amazing Abraham Lincoln, but for all we know, Lincoln could have sounded like Seth Rogen. Who knows?

I wonder what kind of comments Jesus would give the movies we've made about him if he were sitting in the editing room with the directors.

> *"I locked eyes with a Pharisee when I healed that guy. It was pretty defiant."*

> *"There were tears in my eyes when I was talking to her there. My heart was broken."*

> *"Actually, I had a much angrier tone in that moment. People were kind of freaked out."*

"I don't remember being that white or having blue eyes."

"Why do I look so confused? Did my mom forget me at Kmart or something?"

If Jesus and I were sitting in the editing room and going over the stories I've told about him, I wonder what he'd say to me. Have I just preached his message, or have I lived out his story?

When we sacrifice the story for a message, we don't present the full heart of the Gospel. The tension. The joy. The love. The apostle Paul told the Ephesians to be imitators of God. Imitators of the greatest storyteller who still writes the greatest stories.

There are times for sermons and speeches. There are times for debates and discussions. But you have to decide if you want to be a reporter or a storyteller. Reporters give facts and figures and a basic recap of events. I don't believe Jesus is calling us to just be people who memorize and regurgitate his words.

Growing up in church and being involved in youth group meant I went on quite a few retreats. Some retreats were only with our youth group, and some were with students from all over the state or country who would come together for a weekend. It was a great excuse to get out of the house and an even greater excuse for our parents to get us out of the house.

The retreats would have different events and activities mixed in with praise and worship services and preaching. We'd go canoeing, play basketball, or get to watch a band. It just depended on the retreat. It was also a great chance to get to know girls better and find out brand new ways to be ignored. Retreats are great because they give you a chance to separate from your normal routine of life and relax and focus on God. You can cram a lot into a retreat when you don't have to worry about tending to the other needs around your home.

Usually in a weekend we'd go to three or four services and hear a talk from whatever evangelist or pastor was speaking that weekend. The themes of the retreats would vary, but they usually involved pushing us to be more radical with our faith. We'd hear stories about some kid in Pennsylvania who managed to raise $30,000 for missions. Or the kid who got his entire high school saved by throwing anointing oil on everyone who walked by him in the halls. I don't know, it was always something like that.

Usually I'd leave retreats feelings inspired and maybe a bit guilty. We were pushed to share our faith in new and exciting ways, but from what I can remember, it usually seemed like we just needed to be preaching more. To stand up on our lunch tables and call our schools to repentance. "You're an introvert? Tough. Get to preaching, because the world is lost, and it's your fault." I know this was not the intention of most of the speakers, but it could come off that way to me. Then I'd come back home, and it would wear off in time, like a sunburn.

Don't get me wrong, I believe a good, spiritual kick in the pants is necessary at times. We do need to share our faith. We do need to step out and let life get a little awkward. I hear stories every week at my church of how people hear the still, small voice of God calling them to step out in faith and interact with a stranger. After they usually wrestle with, "Is this God or my lunch speaking to me?" they simply step out and start talking to who they feel like they are supposed to. God shows up and lives are impacted, if even for what just seems like a fleeting moment. It matters to the hearers, and it matters to the doers. God is moving all the time in ways we don't understand, or simply don't recognize, and we need to be bold when we feel the push of the Holy Spirit.

I've had moments in my own life where I felt like I was supposed to just go talk to someone. Some I have ignored, and some I have actually followed through on.

I remember seeing this one guy in his early twenties walking around a Starbucks in downtown Ocala, Florida, my hometown, and I felt God wanted me to go talk to him. That's the scary thing about how God seems to push us; he doesn't give us a lot of backstory most times. You just get feeling or a couple of words like, *Go now. Him. Her. You should get a burrito tonight. Steak. Side of queso and chips.* I like to think that last one is God most of the time.

I had watched him walk inside and then back outside. I wasn't exactly sure if he was looking for someone or just killing time. He looked out of place, though. He paced around and then walked away.

I felt like I'd missed my chance. I was upset with myself for being so shy. Then, I tried to rationalize it out and thought, *Maybe you were just feeling like you should talk to him, but it didn't mean anything.*

I asked God to let me see him walk by again and give me a second chance if I'd missed it, kind of hoping God wasn't paying attention to my prayer and that he was busy scrolling through

Facebook instead. Sure enough, ten minutes later he walked by again. He even sat down at the table and chairs outside.

I wish I could tell you I was more spiritually minded than this, but my exact thought was, *Oh crap. I have to actually go do this now.*

I grabbed my coffee cup and walked outside. As I slowly opened the door, I had no clue what I was doing or how to start the conversation.

I thought about being honest and saying, "Hey man, I have been secretly watching you for the past half hour from behind my laptop. I was hoping you wouldn't come back, but now God is making me talk to you."

Instead, I went with, "Hey man, would you like a coffee?" He looked up kind of confused, but accepted my offer.

I went back inside and ordered one and brought it out to him. It had just rained, so I walked outside and wiped off my chair with some napkins like a dainty, old woman.

Turns out, he was pretty easy to talk to. I asked him what he was up to. I found out he was trying to figure out how to see his son and his girlfriend after being in prison for a short time. While he was in prison, his wife decided she'd had enough of it and had started to move on with her life. She didn't want anything to do with him, and he was upset about it. He told me his story, and I mostly just listened.

It was a chilly day, even in Florida, and he was in a T-shirt and jeans. I had an extra jacket in my car, so I asked him if he wanted it. He gladly accepted, even though it was a little short for his arms. I asked him if I could pray with him, and he accepted that offer, too.

And that was it. We shook hands, and I've never seen him again. But I think it mattered.

I believe God is calling us to step out and let life get weird. Jesus said we would receive power through the Holy Spirit, and the book of Acts talks about how the apostles were bold through the power of the Spirit. Honestly, you can't escape the weirdness of the people called by God in the Bible.

Look at John the Baptist, for example. He lived in the desert and ate locusts and honey. Think about that for a second. He was a homeless, insect-eater. Yet, Jesus said, "I tell you the truth, among those born of women, no one has arisen greater than John the Baptist."[4] John was a total freak, and Jesus was a big fan.

We can't get around the weirdness of what it means to truly follow Jesus.

I have a love-hate relationship with arguably the most famous quote of Saint Francis of Assisi. Saint Francis was a Catholic friar of thirteenth century Italy. He is the saint who Pope Francis chose to take his name from. Just plain Francis Assisi, however, sounds like an Italian tennis player.

"Preach the Gospel at all times, if necessary use words."

One of the reasons I hate this saying is because many use it as an excuse to never share their faith. Shy Christians absolutely love this quote. They quote it all the time like it's straight from

Jesus. "I don't have to say anything to anyone ever. I just have to go to church and vote Republican, and I'm good to go. Have I mentioned I wrote a five-star review for Kirk Cameron?" Sometimes we need to use our words. It's part of the gig.

However, I love this quote, because I think it provides some much needed freedom to those who feel condemned by many who have no trouble being loud in public. Not everyone who follows Jesus is called to be a street preacher, and thank God we're not.

One day I was in Moe's Southwest Grill waiting in line for a burrito to destroy my body in ways unimaginable and give me a torture that could only be brought on by the darkest forces of evil in this world, and I saw a guy I recognized from church a few spots ahead of me. I'd never met him, but I knew who he was. We'll just call him Shmark for now.

Shmark was one of those extroverted guys in church services you kind of couldn't miss. I watched him begin his order down the line, and as they were putting toppings on his day-destroying burrito, he asked the worker, "Hey man, do you love Jesus?"

The guy putting his toppings on gave a short chuckle and a side smile and responded by saying, "Uh. Yeah, man." Shmark continued down the assembly line of now likely nervous workers and continued to ask each one if they loved Jesus. One by one they either told him that they did, or they looked at their coworkers giggling, wondering if this guy was serious.

I stood there and watched Shmark get a little weird with everyone. At first, I was impressed. I thought, *Wow, this guy is so bold.*

Then, I felt guilty. *I should be bold enough to do that, too.*

Finally, I felt free. *But maybe God doesn't want us to approach everyone in the exact same way.* Some deep thoughts going on in a Moe's, yet, with all of that in-depth thinking, I never thought, *Hey, maybe I shouldn't be eating this.*

There are a lot of Shmark's in the Christian world. I think we need people like them. We need bold people who have that evangelistic spirit in them. However, they are not all we need. God made you like you are for a reason, and if you can't walk down the line and talk about Jesus, it doesn't mean you are slacking on your witness.

I believe there is danger in being bold just for the sake of being bold when it comes to our faith. It is the same reason you can't just open the Bible, point to a Scripture and say it's a divine Word from the Lord for you or anyone else. Is it the Word of God? Yes. Is it true and good? Yes. But you cannot read the Word of God without the Spirit of God and expect it to be living and active. The Spirit guides us.

Is God calling you to tattoo *Jesus Saves* on your belly and stand on a block in the middle of the city? Cool. Do it.

Is God calling you to build a relationship with your coworkers by being their friend and not giving them a sermon five days a week so that when they need someone to trust, they'll come to you? Cool. Do it.

God is writing a story in each of our lives, and it is not the same story over and over. "Preach the Gospel at all times, if necessary use words." And keep your mind open to how deep the love of God is and how wide his creativity is as well.

When we sacrifice the story for a message, we don't present the full heart of the Gospel.

If we read the Bible and see the sixty-six books as God's completely finished work, we are missing the amazing story he is still writing around us and through us. He's an artist. His writing is meticulous and intricate.

Don't sacrifice the story.

The story is well written. The story is beautiful. The story is full of emotion. The story has plot twists and turns. The story is what draws us in.

Chapter 5

My Public Meltdowns
What Types of People Belong in Church

"Nietzsche famously said, 'Whatever doesn't kill you makes you stronger.' But what he failed to stress is that it almost kills you."[1]

Conan O'Brien

When Jesus spoke about his followers, he said they were the light of the world and a city on a hill that couldn't be hidden.[2] He never intended for the church to be a secret society or an AA meeting.

I believe the church, at its core, wants to be the light of the world. Many of us joined the church because of the hope we found in it. The problem with being the light of the world is I think sometimes we are blinded by the light. "Cut loose like a deuce, another runner in the night,"[3] thus saith Springsteen.

People come into churches broken and messed up, then stop being so outwardly broken and messed up, and then start wondering how people can be so broken and messed up. The light that saved them becomes the same light that blinds them.

There will always be a disconnect when people hold themselves above others. We've all experienced this. Has your boss ever talked down to you? Or maybe the clerk at the DMV? You feel like an idiot. You feel offended. And then you usually feel angry. It is belittling, prideful, and really dependent upon context. Everyone can feel smarter than someone else in any given situation.

It is especially damaging when people come to the church and are immediately separated from it. Damaged, vulnerable, needy, scared, humiliated—these are the kinds of people who are supposed to flood into the church and feel welcomed by it. They can be talked down to like they have issues they shouldn't have anymore. They can be seen as the next project to be fixed, and people go to fixing them right away. When really, all they need right then is to be loved.

They may need to be fixed, but first they probably need to share a meal with someone. They need to matter as a person before their issues need to matter as a project.

Maybe we should stop approaching people with a toolbox and start approaching them with a lunchbox instead.

When I was growing up, we had altars in the front of our church like many did and many still do. I like churches that do, because the entire church is supposed to represent an altar. These altars are meant for prayer. People come and kneel and speak to God, and God speaks to them. I know we can talk with God from anywhere, anytime, but the altars are special. They are a place to pray with a community.

I used to be so embarrassed to go down to the altar during a worship service or even when the pastor would call anyone down who wanted to pray.

"These altars are open for anyone."

I loved hearing that from my pastor, because I wanted people to feel welcomed to pray. Yet, I was still so hesitant to go down to the front.

Why? Because I felt going down to the altar was like waving to the crowd and saying, "Hello, everyone! I have issues! I need help!"

The funny thing is, I was exactly right. That is what it is saying. The problem is the entire congregation should have been going down to the altar, too. We all have issues. We all need help.

Church should be the place where vulnerable people with issues come and feel no judgment. It is the place of hope. A shining city on a hill where people encounter the love of Jesus. The entire church is a giant altar. When I finally came to this realization, I went down to the altar all the time. I couldn't get enough.

Here's why.

I was never at the altar alone. People would come down and kneel next to me. Lay a hand on my shoulder. Sometimes pray silently. Sometimes pray over me. Church people would kneel next to me and share my needs as if they were their own. That's what the term *intercession* means if you've ever heard it used.

When I was 21, my parents got divorced. I was living with both of them that summer when it happened. My sister was working in D.C. during it all, so the weight of my family issues were mine to bear at home.

The day before they separated, the girl I'd been dating for almost two years, and who I wanted to marry, dumped me. I had just said goodbye to her forever and was sitting in my room at my desk. Through the paper-thin walls of our small house, I heard my mom and dad have the conversation I'll never forget.

There was silence. Confusion. Anger.

My entire life had changed in less than 24 hours. It was a one-two punch to my soul.

I sat in my room alone, put my hands over my eyes and sobbed. It was an aching, painful cry. Maybe you know what it feels like. You feel it in your stomach, and it burns all the way up to your throat.

Divorce is a strange demon. There really is no good time in your life for it to happen. When you're a kid, it sucks because you have to bounce around from house to house and meet your parents' new boyfriends and girlfriends. But when you're an adult, you still have to do that, you just have a car and your own place.

When your parents divorce and you're older, you've also had a longer time for life to be established. If you were 5 when it happened, you kind of just grow up with it. Maybe it feels normal. When you're an adult, it feels like your home, your traditions, and everything you know are being ripped away from you.

The hardest part is that you are old enough to recognize the issues and who is wrong and how they are wrong. You see it in a way a child wouldn't be able to understand yet.

Then your parents lean on you for comfort, support, and advice. You can't really pick sides, even though they may assume you've picked a side. Whether they realize it or not, your parents want you to pick a side. But no matter how old you are, you are still their child, and it is devastating.

I was broken, hurting, and lonely that summer. More than I ever had been before. I was trying to be a good son. I was trying to hold it together for my family since my sister was 15 hours away. I was trying to be a therapist, and I had my own break-up to deal with as well.

Some days I was mad at God. Some days all I could do was cry. I had also lost my appetite. I couldn't even finish my burritos. (Actually, that part was probably for the better.)

One Sunday morning at church, I couldn't hold it together. I remember standing during the worship songs unable to fight back the flood of tears. I was surrounded by a crowd but felt like I was on an island by myself. I felt that familiar pain start in my stomach and move its way up to my throat.

"These altars are open for anyone," the pastor reminded us.

I said, "Excuse me," and moved past my friend out into the aisle. I walked down to the altar at the front right side of the church by the side exit doors. I remember thinking about using the doors instead of the altar since I was the only one in the entire church who had just walked down at that point.

I kneeled down, put my head in my folded arms, and began to cry. Not cry—weep. I didn't even say any words. I couldn't. I just wept.

Then, I felt a hand on my right shoulder. I couldn't make out what he was saying, but I knew he was praying for me. I looked out of the corner of my eye and it was a man named Andy, who I honestly didn't really know. We knew who each other was and our families and stuff, but I don't think I'd ever had a conversation with him beyond, "Hey, good morning." And yet, there was Andy kneeling in prayer with me like he was my brother.

I felt a second hand on my left shoulder. This time I didn't hear prayer. I heard crying. Weeping. Kneeling next to me, she seemed to be bearing the same weight as I was in that moment. Intercession.

I'm not sure what drew her down to the altar, but she was there with me in my loneliest moment. I had absolutely no clue then, but seven years later, I would marry that girl on my left.

And there it was, in all of the pain and tears, the beauty of the church. The church as it is meant to shine. Family who would not be family anywhere else. Souls willing to bear the ache and share the tears of someone they don't really even know. They only know Jesus loves them, and so they want to love as well.

When the Spirit moves, that is what he does. He unites us. He binds us together in love.

The church is an altar.

When you think about the heart of the message Jesus preached, and how he was all about love and forgiving people, it's crazy to think he had any enemies. But he did. The Gospels contain many stories of Jesus going toe-to-toe with the Pharisees.

Pharisee seems like a derogatory term nowadays, but they used to be the ones who the people of Israel looked to for spiritual guidance. They were set up to lead the people in the ways and practices of God. Spiritual gurus for the Jews (or Jew-rus?). Experts in every matter of the law.

Yet, they too were blinded by the light. They were meant to bring light to the people and lead in love, but the Pharisees would take the light and use it to oppress the people of Israel. They would put the weight of the law on the Israelites instead of leading them to freedom. They became the law of the land and very powerful. They would oppress the Jews with fear and shame, meanwhile, separating themselves in their pride.

The reason the Pharisees hated Jesus was because he threatened their authority. Jesus came in preaching the opposite of oppression from the law they had been manipulating to increase their power, and instead, preached a message of love and freedom—two traits the Pharisees did not possess.

Jesus' first big speech in a synagogue began by him quoting from the book of Isaiah:

> *"The Spirit of the Lord is upon me,*
> *Because He has anointed Me*
> *To preach the gospel to the poor;*
> *He has sent me to heal the brokenhearted,*
> *To proclaim liberty to the captives*
> *And recovery of sight to the blind,*
> *To set at liberty those who are oppressed;*
> *To proclaim the acceptable year of the Lord."*

Luke 4:18-19

He found the beauty and freedom of the law and came to release his people from the oppression of the Pharisees.

So here steps in Mr. Forgiveness and Love, challenging the words of God they had manipulated to the people, and thus challenging their authority. The people also loved him because he was healing everyone and giving out free food and wine. Jesus was kind of the perfect party guest.

The Pharisees were given a responsibility by God and had completely warped it to meet their needs and to give them power over the people they were put in place to serve. They had taken the light of the faith and become blinded by it, blinded to their own sin, and blinded to the heart and the hope of it.

One day, the Pharisees brought a woman caught in adultery before Jesus to have him judge her. They said she needed to be stoned. It was a set up to trap him in his words, but Jesus saw it coming.

She was put before him in her sin. Probably barely dressed. Probably in pain from being arrested. Probably in tears as men stood and decided her fate. She was a woman with issues in front of a crowd at the altar of Jesus.

Jesus stooped to the ground, wrote in the dirt, and then said to the Pharisees, "He who is without sin among you, let him throw a stone at her first." One by one, from the oldest to the youngest, the Pharisees began to walk away. She was not going to die in her sin that day.

When they had all left, Jesus looked at her and asked her, "Where are those accusers of yours? Has no one condemned you?"

She said, "No one, Lord."

Then Jesus replied, "Neither do I condemn you; go and sin no more."[4]

She came to the altar with issues, and left with compassion and freedom.

Jesus then said to the crowd watching, "I am the light of the world. He who follows me shall not walk in darkness, but have the light of life."[5]

The light, our hope, is not in systems and practices of a church or the established authorities. The Light of the World is Jesus.

At the altar of Jesus, you will not find oppression and a weight of rules. You will find compassion, freedom, and redemption.

As I said earlier, the summer of my parents' divorce was a dark time for me. I was also still dealing with the break-up. I was heartbroken and unable to shake off the pain. I desperately wanted it not to affect me like it was, or even just become numb to it. I would try to sleep, and then I would dream about it. I couldn't really escape.

During that time, I was a janitor at my church in Ocala doing odd jobs. After the Wednesday night youth service, I was supposed to set up lunch tables and trashcans for the school that had lunch in there the next day.

One night after the service, I saw my ex and a mix of emotions was triggered in me as the weight of the summer became too much for me to keep inside anymore. I was never one for making a scene. I was the type of guy who would usually just go to his room and cry, but this summer had changed me in many ways.

As I was getting the lunchroom in order, the trashcans were not so much being set up; they were being thrown across the room. I was pretty much having a Jerry Maguire meltdown. The youth group students were scurrying out and avoiding eye contact with me as I flung the trashcans and tables around. I started to run out of the room in a blur of anger.

Before I could make it out the front doors, I was stopped. I felt a hand grab my arm tightly and not let go. She was a woman who is not even five feet tall, but had a grip like a python. It was my fifth grade teacher, Mrs. Carte, who had watched me grow up.

I literally tried to break free and sling my arm out, but again she wouldn't let go. I yelled at her to let me go. You know how you have those sentences that don't really make any sense because you're so angry? It's just a lot of nonsense. The frustration had overcome me, and I was saying a lot in anger and pain. I continued demanding that she let me go. But she wouldn't.

She brought me back over to the very tables I had shoved across the floor and we sat down. My friend Luke and I were initially going to go to a movie that night so he was there, too, and came and sat with us. I could see on his face he was concerned, and he and his family had been there for my other emotional breakdowns which were not in public. I spent a lot of nights at Luke's house that summer just trying to run away from it all. Mrs. Carte's husband Robert ended up joining us as well. And after coming by and noticing the situation, my friend Nick, the children's pastor, stopped and sat down with us, too.

There I was with four people surrounding me. No one chastised me for not controlling my anger. No one came down on me with Bible verses about how I needed to be over it by now or how I needed to forgive anyone.

I didn't get a lesson; I got listened to. Four people stopped their lives for me that night, and it changed me.

Robert shared some stories with me about confusing times in his past. Mrs. Carte told me that Robert had broken up with her before they got married. It was a tough time for their young relationship, but there they were sharing it in confidence, and even laughing about it. She reminded me of what David wrote in Psalm 37, about how if you trust in the Lord, he will endure with you and give you the desires of your heart.

We talked for over an hour. They understood why I was frustrated and hurt. They surrounded me in love. They reminded me of who I am through Christ and how God will use all of the pain for good.

We prayed together, and I locked up the church. Luke and I went on to go see a movie.

That night was such a perfect picture to me of what the church is meant to be. A place where issues are put on display, and you are welcomed. You are welcome to be loved and to heal. A place where we share one another's burdens at the altar.

I could have been condemned, but I was consoled.

I could have been rebuked, but I was restored.

Do you remember how super frustrating it was as a kid when your parents would tell you to do something they were not doing themselves? You know, because as kids we knew everything. We'd say, "Why do I have to do it? You're not doing it?"

And parents would respond with, "Do as I say, not as I do."

The Pharisees were all about doing as they said and not as they did. They would look in the mirror and see perfection, and then look everywhere else and see sin.

It's like that episode of *Seinfeld* where George thinks he can see without his glasses when he squints.

> *GEORGE: What, you're gonna take her word over mine? I'm your best friend!*
>
> *JERRY: Yeah, but you're blind as a bat!*
>
> *GEORGE: I was squinting! Remember that drive from Wortsborough? I was spotting those raccoons.*
>
> *JERRY: They were mailboxes, you idiot. I didn't have the heart to tell you.*[6]

The Pharisees had a Costanza complex. Pride clouds your vision and has you see yourself differently than what is truly there. Jesus referred to them as a bowl that looks clean on the outside but is filthy on the inside.

When I was working in the Washington, D.C. metro area, I lived in a section of Arlington called Crystal City. It is right over the Potomac River from D.C. on the blue and yellow Metro line. Crystal City sounds like it belongs in *The Wizard of Oz* or *Breaking Bad,* but it actually is a nice place and very quiet at night.

Crystal City was about three Metro stops away from Arlington Cemetery on your way into the District, so I went by there often and always took visiting friends. It is quite a sight to see there, and if you've never been, you've probably at least seen pictures. Thousands and thousands of white tombstones of our fallen soldiers as far as you can see. JFK's grave is there with the eternal flame burning, as well as the Tomb of the Unknown Soldier. It's all humbling, moving, and also beautiful.

Many people go there and take pictures. It's easy to get lost in the beauty of the landscape and forget what it actually is—a cemetery. Many people would never go through a graveyard in their city, much less take pictures of it. Yet, Arlington Cemetery so easily becomes a tourist stop and photo op.

In Matthew 23, Jesus really starts laying into the Pharisees. It's no wonder that three chapters later they arrest him.

> *"Woe to you, teachers of the law and Pharisees, you hypocrites! You are like whitewashed tombs, which look beautiful on the outside but on the inside are full of the bones of the dead and everything unclean. In the same way, on the outside you appear to people as righteous but on the inside you are full of hypocrisy and wickedness."*

The Pharisees would look at themselves the way tourists see Arlington Cemetery. The difference between the Pharisees and Jesus was not actually their doctrines, because Jesus never spoke against the Hebrew law. The difference was their hearts. Their compassion. The Pharisees had none.

When Jesus spoke with people who needed help, their sin was usually the last thing he would address. Instead, he would have compassion on them, heal them, and then he would give them a command.

When the Pharisees brought the adulterous woman to be stoned, Jesus had compassion on her. He freed her, and the last thing he told her was to "go and sin no more." Jesus would make an investment into their lives before he would give them a command.

There are a lot of people who want to give out advice, because it makes them feel smart, or they may genuinely be trying to help. But there are not a lot of people willing to make the investment in a life. I have a hard time listening to advice from someone who I first of all didn't ask for any advice from, and secondly, who has not made an investment into my life.

Compassion leads to change. Change opens the door for a command.

Compassion. Change. Command.

> As Jesus and his disciples were leaving Jericho, a large crowd followed him. Two blind men were sitting by the roadside, and when they heard that Jesus was passing by, they shouted, "Lord, Son of David, have mercy on us!"
>
> The crowd rebuked them and told them to be quiet, but they shouted all the louder, "Lord, Son of David, have mercy on us!"
>
> Jesus stopped and called them. 'What do you want me to do for you?' he asked.
>
> "Lord," they answered, "we want our sight."
>
> Jesus had compassion on them and touched their eyes. Immediately they received their sight and followed him.
>
> Matthew 20:29-34

Jesus had compassion on the men, healed them, and then they followed him. The Pharisees would begin with a command. Many people in the church begin with commands and wonder why no one is experiencing the love of God. No one can experience the love of God if his people lack his compassion.

I think sometimes it is difficult for us to see God as a loving God who rejoices over his creation when the people who should represent him the best do the most finger pointing. The light of the world was never meant to blind the church and bind us in rules.

You may have heard the saying, "One must belong before they believe, and believe before they behave." I really like this way of thinking. Most people desire community in some way or another. How else do you explain CrossFit? Who would endure CrossFit training if they were by themselves? It's insane.

Community is vital to the church. Whenever I have moved to a new city, I immediately try to plug into a local church for community. Once you leave your hometown or college town, making friends can be quite challenging. If it's up to me to make friends through my work or just randomly on the street, I'm usually out of luck. I find a church I think fits my stage in life well enough, and then I go to as many events as I can. It's awkward for a while, but then it only takes one person and everything can change. I can remember a few people who reached out to me when I moved to a new city, and they changed my life by opening up a new community of friends.

People desire community, and if they can't get it in church, they will look elsewhere. Many churches fail to see change in their congregations, because they lack community, and people feel like they do not belong. The church is designed to go through changes as a unit—as one body.

You know what happens when only part of the body is experiencing change? It looks like those guys at the gym who only work out the top halves of their bodies. They put all of their energy into their chest and arms and forget about their legs. You'll see many of them waddling around the gym like penguins. Have you ever been to a church and thought, *Hmmm . . . I'm getting a strong penguin vibe in here.* Well, now you know why.

The arms need the legs to be changing at the same rate. The times I have felt the most spiritual growth in my life have been the times I've felt most loved by a community. The churches that usually see the most growth have been the ones who love their communities the most.

Who are you when you come to church? Who do you think you have to be?

Look again at who Jesus said he had come for. Do they sound like people who have it together?

"The Spirit of the Lord is upon Me,
Because He has anointed Me
To preach the gospel to the poor;
He has sent Me to heal the brokenhearted,
To proclaim liberty to the captives
And recovery of sight to the blind,
To set at liberty those who are oppressed;
To proclaim the acceptable year of the Lord."[7]

The church is an altar. It is meant to be the place where the weak are made strong. Where the hopeless find hope. Where the broken are restored. It was never meant to be the place where the strong only meet with the strong. We are all in need. It's just a question of if we realize it yet or not.

Chapter 6

Chili's, Bennigan's, and Other Places I Wasn't Allowed to Go
How My Mom Conquered Her Fear of Bar-and-Grills

"Well, you can't never let anything happen to him. Then nothing would ever happen to him. Not much fun for little Harpo."[1]

Finding Nemo

Ohio is an interesting place. I've been there four times in my life. One of my best friends, Brandon, lives near Canton, so I try to visit him whenever I get the chance. He's the same guy that watched me run my leg into the pool drain in 4th grade.

A "short drive" in Ohio is usually at least 45 minutes. I learned this on one of my visits when Brandon told me a music store was a short drive away. As we drove past endless cornfields, we discussed the conundrum that is Ohio.

"I often wonder who were the first people to live in Ohio," Brandon said. "Someone said, 'Hey, this place is freezing cold 98 percent of the year. There are no beautiful mountains, and everything is a billion miles away. Let's set up shop here.'"

Ohioans have a Midwestern kindness to them that seems lost in so many other places of the country. Its pace is slow like the South and most places you go have the small-town feel. There is a remarkable number of people from Ohio who end up in Florida. I guess they don't want to lose the joy of being in a swing state.

Even though I've never lived there, I guess I have Ohio roots. Both of my parents are from there. They followed my mom's parents down from Toledo, and for some reason, ended up in Ocala.

My mom was the youngest of six children, all raised in a Christian Missionary Alliance church. She grew up with a strong reverence for the church and strict adherence to its rules. They were not even allowed to eat any food inside the church walls. If they were going to have ice cream or something, it had to be outside on the steps at least. Food inside the church was the first sign of secularism. I wonder how they justified communion, though.

My mom's cultural upbringing in the church left her with a desire to change later on in adulthood. But much like a short drive in Ohio, these personal changes took her quite a long time to get to.

Many Christians grow up with a warped, holy fear instilled in them by their church. However, I don't think the church puts fear in people's minds the way it works in *The Hunger Games* or anything. Some people believe religion intentionally walls people in with fear, and while that may be true of some religions,

I don't believe it is the case with every Christian church you could walk into on a Sunday morning. At least not the ones I've encountered.

I believe churches instill fear in their congregations in one or more of the following three ways:

1) *Trying to push them towards holiness*

A lot of the fear comes from a well-intentioned place of trying to help people live better Christian lives. The Bible talks a lot about fleeing from sin and the things of the world and pursuing Christ.

True, these instructions were meant to challenge believers, but ultimately it was to set them free. Unfortunately, the church can turn messages meant for freedom into messages of condemnation.

Guilt should have no place in the Gospel, but fear usually accompanies guilt. Guilt is like the French fries of the church. It comes with everything, and it's not healthy.

2) *They are fearful themselves.*

In the words of the great philosopher Yul Brynner from *Cool Runnings*, "We're different. People are always afraid of what's different."[2] A lot of people who have grown up in the church have never really been outside of it. Sure, they'll go to the store or the gym every now and then and have a conversation with a stranger, or do a church outreach day, but they never really leave the culture. They go to a Christian elementary school through Christian high school, then attend a Christian college, and then start working for a church.

This isn't wrong, and I know many well-adjusted people who grew up this way. You don't have to necessarily be raised like this to be fearful of the world.

My grandparents described themselves as "partiers" back in their day. It's hard to imagine your grandparents doing a keg-stand. It may be hard to imagine your grandparents doing anything at all. But even with their partying pasts, my grandparents were the ones who raised my mom in the fear of the church. They had been so outside of the church that once they experienced the grace of God, they ran full steam into the church like a white lady to a sale at the Gap.

Growing up, I was only surrounded by the church culture. I went to a small Christian school until 8th grade, and my best friends were my church peers. I don't regret it; however, I was fearful of the things of the world. I had been warned my entire life about "the world." I was told when I got to high school or college that I would constantly be tempted by the people of the world to do drugs and spit on a picture of Christ. I was also going to be challenged in my faith by godless professors who would flunk me for believing in a Higher Power or being unwilling to come to class naked. None of that happened, and I went to the University of Florida and even minored in religion.

Still, I kept my guard up knowing in any moment of weakness, the devil could take me down. I lived in fear. Fear of falling into the arms of the world. Fear of angering God and leading people astray.

3) Pride

Pride is probably the most influential sin in the world, followed by selfishness. I suppose you could even say selfishness is an act of pride. The majority of arguments are caused by pride. Pride warps your vision. You see yourself as better than you really are, and you see others as worse than they really are. Pride is always in competition, and its measuring stick is itself.

Pride instills fear in others by looking down its nose at them, and reminding them holiness is based on works, not on grace. Christians who are full of pride are often disgusted with the things of the world, but only the visible things. Sins like gossip, selfishness, and anger are more justifiable somehow.

It's funny how pride and insecurity go hand-in-hand. You wouldn't think they would, but they do.

If someone else has a job you want, your insecurity says you'll never get a position like that because you're not good enough, while your pride is saying you deserve it because of how loyal you've been to the company. Both are at work at the same time.

Pride delivers a message of condemnation and fear disguised as concern.

My parents are interesting people. I remember realizing they were just making it up as they went along when it came to raising us. No parent knows what they are doing. I look back on some of their decisions in raising us and think, "What was that about?"

Every parent has a weird set of rules. Some rules are made for no real reason at all, but many are made from honestly trying to do what's best for your family. Many are a result of fear. And if you're in the church, many rules are a result of the fear the church put in you.

I wasn't allowed to watch *The Simpsons* or *Scooby-Doo*, which I guess is understandable. I also wasn't allowed to watch *The*

Smurfs either, and I still don't really know why on that one. These shows were off-limits, but I remember watching *Cheers* and *Night Court* with my parents. And going to see the *Naked Gun* movies in theaters (which I'm sure were much worse than *The Smurfs*).

This double standard puzzled me for years, but I think I've finally figured out my parents' reasoning. They didn't let me watch shows they didn't want to have to sit there and watch with me. It's really quite genius. I'm totally going to use it on my kids. "No, you're not watching *Dora the Explorer*! She's talking to that monkey with her witchcraft-voodoo, and I will have none of that in my house! You're going to watch TV with me. Turn on *Scrubs*." Seriously, it's genius.

We weren't allowed to go trick-or-treating either. Instead, we went to Hallelujah Night at the church, or you may know it as Harvest Festival. This was the church's alternative to the evil of dressing up in costumes and getting candy door-to-door by having the kids come to church dressed up in costumes and get candy.

Many of us Christian kids wanted to go trick-or-treating so badly, but we had to settle for a little activity I call "reverse trick-or-treating," which is when you hand out tracts door-to-door. And there is no candy. There are no costumes. There is no fun.

Now I'm not complaining, because I always had a lot of fun at Hallelujah Harvest Halloworship Festival Night. We had fun games, and I always got a ton of candy. Plus, my friends were there. I just don't see how it was really any better than trick-or-treating. Parents saw it as a healthy alternative to Halloween and another chance to bring people inside of our church walls.

I remember dressing up like a clown one year (not sure how I picked that costume or who picked it for me—perhaps another example of my mom making things up as she went), but I remember hating it because the plastic nose hurt my face, and I hated wearing make-up. After that, I went as a "Soldier in God's Army" decked out in camouflage overalls, T-shirt, and headband.

My mom and I got lazy, and I went as the same soldier for about five years in a row, which probably explains why my costumes always suck for Halloween to this day. I always choose them by looking in my closet and saying to myself, "All right, what do I already have that I could pass off as a costume without having to buy anything or spend any amount of energy on it? Plaid shirts and jeans. Looks like I'm going as a cowboy again. Giddy up." It's not that I hate holiday spirit. I do enjoy the parties. I've just been terrible at costumes since I was a kid, and now you know why.

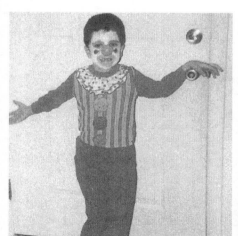 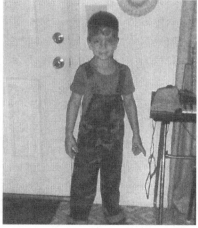

You can see why we went with the soldier one.

Many Christians even went as far as to boycott Disney. Launched in 1996 by the American Family Association, the boycott called for all Christians to avoid Disney movies, merchandise, and especially the theme parks due to what the AFA described as "a decline in moral and family values from the days of founder Walt Disney."[3] This was bad news to Christian kids everywhere, especially kids like me who grew up 90 minutes from Orlando.

I have to give it to my parents on this one, because we never boycotted anything Disney. We went to the parks, watched the movies, and memorized the songs. Some of my favorite memories are watching my dad eat his way through the Magic Kingdom.

> *"You kids want ice cream?"*
> *"YEAH!"*
> *"All right let's get some!"*

> Twenty minutes later . . .

> *"You guys want ice cream?"*
> *"No, we're full."*
> *"All right let's get some!"*

> Repeat.

There is always an opportunity to boycott a company in the minds of some conservative Christian groups. And while I want to believe it comes from a well-meaning place in their hearts, I now believe it is mostly a result of fear driven by pride. They are willing to believe a lie, and their pride is blinding them.

All children have selective hearing. Kids are like dogs who only respond to a few words, like *treat*, *food*, and *Xbox*. So I don't remember a lot of conversations verbatim from when I was young, more so, just random snippets of life as it happened around me.

My dad can talk for years on end, even if no one is listening. I've never worried about him becoming an old man just muttering to himself in the park. He may end up talking to himself in the park, but he'll at least be having in-depth conversations about the state of affairs in the Middle East.

My mom is a good talker and a good listener. My sister is a talker, too. I remember being so happy when she finally got a cell phone and I didn't have to keep answering her phone calls at the house. I'd answer the phone dozens of times a day hoping someone would possibly be calling me:

"Hello?"

"Melissa?"

"Hold on I'll get her."

As the little brother, people often thought I was her when I answered, which was a nice shot to the confidence I already lacked. I'm certain many other little brothers can relate.

It's tough being the youngest in the family. You're usually fighting for attention and for someone to notice you amongst all the busyness of their lives and their conversations. It's no wonder the majority of comedians are the youngest of their siblings. Look it up. Dave Chappelle. Billy Crystal. Ellen DeGeneres. Jim Carrey. Eddie Murphy. Tina Fey. Stephen Colbert—youngest of eleven! This trait is so prevalent because the youngest always have to figure out a way to get noticed, and usually will try anything.

My sister is four years older than me, so she was able to have actual conversations with my parents that usually went over my head. I'd sit in the backseat and listen. Some stuff would stick and some wouldn't. Selective hearing and selective understanding.

One statement in particular stands out to me, even after all these years. My sister and I were riding in the back of our 1975 Chrysler Cordoba. If you've never seen a Cordoba, just imagine a 1940s mob car mixed with your grandma's Buick and metal seatbelt buckles sure to burn a hole through your arm on a sunny Florida day. The thing was a tank. We'd cram in the backseat and pray to God the A/C was working that day.

I remember being in the back of the Cordoba and driving by a Bennigan's restaurant on Highway 40 in Ocala. (It's no longer open, but I think 90% of my friends worked there at some point.) On the sign it said, "Bennigan's Grill & Tavern." My mom saw the sign and said in a huff, "That place is terrible. They disguise the bar with a restaurant. It's so deceptive."

Like I said, we weren't closed off in a bubble or anything. We went to Disney World and watched Mel Brooks movies, but there were some places that irked my mom, and Bennigan's Grill & Tavern was one of those places she took a stand against. And Chili's. I remember driving by Chili's, dying to go inside, as we drove to Piccadilly, yet again, to watch the senior citizens take out their teeth and put them on the table.

This was back when restaurants like Chili's really started blowing up all over the place. They were all exactly the same, just with a different flair. Ruby Tuesday. TGI Friday's. Applebee's. Texas Roadhouse. All of those places where the food isn't really good, but it's not fast food. Somewhere right in between. They're like the Hootie & the Blowfish of restaurants. As an elementary school kid, these were the places to go for your birthday dinner, and we weren't allowed to go.

Jesus described false prophets as wolves in sheep's clothing. They play dress up and masquerades as something they are not.[4] My mom equated these bar-and-grills to that same analogy. It starts off all nice, like, "Hey, come on in for some mediocre food and heart disease," and then you get one glimpse of the bar in the corner and BAM! You're an alcoholic. Oh, we're on to you, Chili's.

Now, if my mom had said, "We're not eating at Chili's, because I care about your health and well-being, and I don't want to subject your intestines to torture unimaginable in the form of what they're trying to pull off as Mexican food," it would have made a lot of sense. But that wasn't the reason. We were avoiding it to keep our witness intact, and because it felt morally wrong to my parents.

I never went to Chili's until we started going to lunch with our pastor and his family every Sunday when I was about 10 years old. They delivered us to the promised land of bar-and-grills.

How ironic is it that my mom now attends a church which meets at a bar-and-grill in South Florida? She was just eating breakfast there one morning and heard some people singing a worship song she recognized. She walked over and discovered it was a church service. She has now been attending for years. Her pastor is okay with her hypocrisy.

My mom looks back on those days and what we rejected and says she feels foolish. I don't fault her though. She was figuring it out as she went, and it takes time to finally settle into some areas of your faith. You can take the girl out of Ohio, but you can't take the legalistic-Ohio-fear out of the girl.

Ohio is a lot like faith. It's easy to get lost. And everything is spread out and takes a while to get to.

When a movement gains momentum, it often progresses down an unorganized, undefined path. Its proponents may know where they want to go, but not necessarily how to get there. And in the process, they take on more than they can handle. Like ordering your first burrito at Chipotle.

There is usually a period of overcorrection. Robin Williams talked about this idea when it comes to acting. He said he would do many takes for the same scene and start out kind of placid, then expand it from there. There was usually a point in the takes where he and the director knew, "All right, that's a little too far," and he'd come back down and settle on somewhere in the middle. It sometimes takes a process of overcorrection before you can settle on the best scene or course of action.[5]

It's true of all churches, and people in general. We grow. We evolve. We learn new ideas and facts. We change our minds. We isolate ourselves; then we overexert ourselves. It's all part of the process of life and figuring out how we want to live, who we want to be, and where the healthy balance is.

It's all integral to our faith. There's an ancient Italian maxim which says, "He who is resistant to change is destined to perish." I wish I could tell you I learned that in college or in my private studies, but the truth is I heard it in the movie *Hot Rod*.

It's a process. We should be changing our minds. I have noticed that the unhappiest people are the ones who have not embraced the changes in their lives. They want it to be like it was in high school, or like when they were kids, but life doesn't stay the same. Especially in religion. Old fundamentalists say, "It ain't like it used to be!" They are cranky, stagnant, and doing jack squat for God. Stuck in your ways, or longing for your old glory days, is a miserable way to live.

There was a point in time when many people were strongly against interracial marriage. Even some pastors would point to verses in the Bible and say, "See? God is against it!" Some churches were against desegregation during the Civil Rights Movement of the 1960s. Not all of them, but many of them. And now some of my best friends are African Americans. We speak of these ideas like they are distant history, because the pictures are black and white, but it was not long ago at all. It's scary to think of how close it is in history, but also encouraging to know change can come. And yes, we still have a long way to go.

It makes me wonder what else the church must overcorrect itself on in order to evolve. It's a process. And it's a process that God knows exists.

Apostle Paul talks about a process inside all of us when it comes to faith.

> *And we also thank God continually because, when you received the word of God, which you heard from us, you accepted it not as a human word, but as it actually is, the word of God, which is indeed at work in you who believe.*
>
> *1 Thessalonians 2:13*

The Word of God is at work. We haven't learned everything we're going to learn about it. God is a sculptor with a hammer and chisel. He is a God of process and refining.

There was a song I used to sing when I was a kid. I still remember singing it and acting out the motions along with my peers. It bears truth and is a good reminder, but it also has an Orwellian, big-brother feel to it.

O be careful little feet where you go,
O be careful little feet where you go,
For the Father up above is looking down in love,
So be careful little feet where you go.

The verses would change to "eyes what you see," and so on. It wasn't exactly "Here I Am to Worship," but it got the job done. Kids all over the world sing this song. And it's true; we should be careful. But I think it could be one of those songs parents want their kids singing to help keep their kids a little bit scared of acting up. The phrase "God is watching you" really depends on how you spin it.

> *"God is watching you, and he is looking out for you*
> *and loves you, little one."*

> *"God is watching you, and he can't wait for you to*
> *screw up so he can punish you, punk."*

I think a lot of kids in the church grow up with an image of God reflecting the latter of those two. We know God loves us and is big and mighty, even good, but we still have a fear lingering in our minds. A fear of this God who is looking down, in love, but who is disappointed in us. Almost like a father you will never be good enough for. So we put much more effort and energy into serving the church trying to make God happy and earn his love back.

It's even a mentality I carry with me to this day that I'm still trying to shake off. I know I am not saved by works but by grace, but I still get worried God will not like me as much or will not bless me as much if I slack off or stumble in sin. I find myself fearful of the Father up above looking down in love.

I think a fear of the Lord is healthy. Proverbs says, "The fear of the Lord is the beginning of knowledge."[6] People can translate *fear* however they want to and say it means *respect* or *admiration*, and that's fine. But Paul blatantly says in Romans, "So do not become proud, but fear."[7] A little fire under your seat is not a bad thing. He's God, and he is a judge. It's not something we should take lightly. However, if our focus is to move towards God out of fear, we are missing the romance. One of the biggest revelations I've had is so simple I can't believe it took me so long to get it.

God loves me because he loves me.

That's it. There is nothing I can do to earn it. There is nothing I can do to lose it. God loves me because I am his.

We lose sight of the extent of God's love when we are more focused on a Father who looks down on us in disappointment. It may come from a good message of fearing God and fleeing sin, but it can easily get too religious and stick with us in subconscious, dangerous ways.

In an effort to please God, we move in fear instead of love. We've got much more overcorrecting to do.

Chapter 7

Zacchaeus
How God Burst My Church Bubble

"It's a topsy-turvy world, and maybe the problems of two people don't amount to a hill of beans. But this is our hill. And these are our beans."[1]

The Naked Gun

When I was a kid I always liked going to church for the most part. I even enjoyed Sunday school. It's not a popular activity anymore, but Sunday school was where you went an hour before the main Sunday morning service. It was the appetizer. The chips and queso. (If I order it, will you guys have some?) It was also a great way to get a few extra reading assignments to do outside of regular school. The nerds loved it.

Still, when I was a kid I enjoyed going. There was a point in time when I was the only one in my family who went to Sunday school, and my mom would reward me for being the holiest in our house by swinging by Dunkin' Donuts on the way there. My mom and I had a special morning-drive bond, because we did it so often together. We'd get Coffee Coolatta's and chocolate glazed donuts. She'd drop me off at the height of my sugar rush and then hang around the foyer chatting with other moms dodging Sunday school.

I learned a lot in those mornings and had some wonderful teachers. We were taught a ton of music along with the "O Be Careful Little Feet" song, like the "I Am a C-H-R-I-S-T-I-A-N" song. This song was a great way to learn how to spell and perhaps a precursor to Gwen Stefani's B-A-N-A-N-A-S thing. I loved watching kids trying to sing it faster and faster until they turned blue in the face. I always wanted to see someone pass out while singing it, but I never did. Maybe someday.

"Father Abraham" was another one. Father Abraham had many sons. Apparently I am one of them, and so are you. It was essentially a song about rapid breeding.

We also sang a song about Zacchaeus. Maybe you've heard it. It was kind of offensive to short people. And redundant. But we sang it nonetheless.

> *Zacchaeus was a wee, little man,*
> *And a wee, little man was he.*
> *He climbed up in a sycamore tree,*
> *For the Lord he wanted to see.*
> *And as the Savior came that way,*
> *He looked up in the tree,*
> *And he said, "Zacchaeus, you come down,"*
> *For I'm going to your house today.*

This song became more personal to me the older I got and the less I grew in stature. I started to worry one day people would write a song about how I had to stand on a stepstool to reach the cups on the top shelf in my kitchen. And kids would do the hand motions of me reaching up like a toddler for the cookie jar.

Even so, the Zacchaeus song was fun to sing and we all liked it. It was cute and told part of the story. I know it's a kids' song, but it really left out some important details.

Yes, there was a man named Zacchaeus who climbed up a sycamore tree to see Jesus, and Jesus went to his house with him. That part is accurate. But this song only tells part of the story.

The fact is Zacchaeus was a tax collector in Jericho, which means most people probably hated him or tried to avoid him.

Let's have a little Jewish history lesson here. Now, I'm not a rabbi, but I do know some Yiddish words: *Oy vey! Mensch. Kibosh.* And various other ones Robin Williams used in *Mrs. Doubtfire.*

In the days of Zacchaeus, Israel was under Roman rule. If you visit Rome today, you will see mainly tourists taking selfies with fake guards holding plastic swords, but back in the day Rome was no joke.

The elite rulers were oppressive, scary, and obsessed with wearing bedsheets as clothing. The Jews weren't exactly in love with them. They weren't the Olive Garden kind of Italians, where "When you're here, you're family." It was more like, "We're here, we're severe, get used to it. Give me your breadsticks."

Every once in a while, a Jew would get a lucky break and somehow get on the good side of the Romans. Some Jews, like Zacchaeus, were allowed to become tax collectors. They were employed by the Romans to collect taxes from their own people.

Tax collectors would sell out their friends and rob them, too. They were notorious for overcharging and getting rich off of the extra cash. It took a lot of chutzpah. (I thought of another Yiddish word.)

Zacchaeus was a terrible person. Plain and simple. He had to climb a tree to see Jesus because A) he was a wee, little man, and B) nobody was going to make any space for him in the crowd.

He wasn't misunderstood. He wasn't an outcast. He was a bad guy. And he knew it.

I graduated college in 2009 during the throes of the recession. I started working everyone's dream job—parking cars at a hospital. It was a major disappointment, because I had been told my whole life I could be anything I wanted to be. And then I found out I actually couldn't. I had a degree in advertising but no work experience and no connections. No one was hiring. No one except the valet at the hospital, which was located in my college town of Gainesville, Florida.

I didn't really know what I was doing there. I had thought God would have had a bigger and better plan for me, at least something a little sexier than a blue polo shirt, tacky khaki shorts, and white socks. It was humiliating at times. Infuriating at others. I would get in some of the most disgusting cars owned by the most disgusting people. Fast food and trash all over the floor. A dip can in the middle cup holder. One time I literally had cockroaches crawl over my lap.

I begged God to get me out of there every day, but I never got another job offer in those two years.

Turns out, I was right where I needed to be.

Up until then, I'd mostly been around my church friends in my church bubble doing church activities. I had a desire to reach people outside of the church, but I just thought it would be better if they came to my church instead of me going to where they were. You know, out in the "mission field."

But then, God brought me to the valet.

The type of crowd I had managed to avoid throughout my college experience had now become the people I spent 40 hours a week with.

Gainesville is a college town and most of the valet employees were still in college, and they did what college kids do. I'd not gone to many bars in college. To be honest, I was kind of terrified of them. At one point in my life, I thought if you had beer in public then you completely ruined your witness. I told people that, too. When your mom is boycotting Chili's, I guess the logic can trickle down to the kids.

But as I said, I was with a new crowd. I liked my coworkers and wanted to be liked in return. So when I got invited to parties, I went. And I had a lot of fun.

I'll never forget one night when I left a Christian hangout because a couple girls from the valet had invited me out to a bar with everyone from work. I felt bad leaving the church group, but I wanted to go be with this new group of people I was falling in love with.

I walked into the dive bar and my friend from the valet, Eric, turned and saw me, stood up on the booth, lifted his beer and yelled, "Jon!" I was welcomed. I was accepted. No one said, "Hey, aren't you supposed to be a Christian? What are you doing here? Ready to ruin your witness?" At that moment, I realized I wasn't under the judgment and scrutiny of these people. I was in friendship. They were just thrilled I was there with them. They wanted me to hang out and have a beer. That's it.

I started going out a lot more with friends from work, and I didn't even have to hide my faith. My faith came up in many conversations, and without me even having to look them in the eyes and ask them if they knew where they would spend eternity. Surprisingly, I found out that many people are more curious about religion than the church gives them credit for, but they aren't going to pour their hearts out to a random dude yelling on the side of a street.

I was having amazing conversations and seeing more spiritual fruit than I'd ever seen in my life. Some valet friends were coming to church with me, even asking me about it without me bringing it up first. And I was having a blast hanging out with them. I wasn't flawless through it all (I never have been), but it was an amazing time because I was in a territory I'd never been allowed to go to before. Territory I never allowed myself to go to.

God brought me to the valet.

This wasn't exactly popular with some of my Christian friends, and I caught some flack. I had people sharply disagree with my new activities. I had friends tell me I was falling away from God. I saw some worried eyes looking at me.

Some Christians will say, "Well, I'm just concerned." Or "Well, I'm just praying for you." When the truth is, they are really saying, "Well, I'm judging you."

And let's not kid ourselves, sometimes we need to be judged. Sometimes we need rebuke. Sometimes we need our best friends to punch us in the face. I'm grateful I have people in my life who are willing to do so. But in this situation, they were wrong. They weren't there with me. They weren't friends with my new friends. They were not living in my story.

It made me think about my reputation in a new way. I think we should protect our names. Your name, or your reputation, is important. Your witness is important. And sometimes we fall.

Still, I looked at the good I was seeing, and I looked at my reputation. I wondered if I would have to choose between the two at some point.

Could I cross the line over to the world and disappoint the church? Did I have to cross a line? Which was worth more: my name or souls?

This is when I started to walk the tightrope between the church and the world for the first time in my life.

Jesus didn't exactly get a pat on the back from the religious folks when he told Zacchaeus he wanted to go to his house. Zacchaeus wasn't just a secret sinner. His sins were out in the open. Jesus was a rabbi and a teacher in the synagogue. If he sat down and ate with a tax collector, he would be putting his reputation on the line.

You may not have grown up in church or may not have been involved in church, but religious pressure is very real, and it is intimidating. It's bad enough in 21st century United States, but back in Jesus' day, the religious leaders were also the law keepers. Jesus wasn't just under pressure that some people may not like him; he was under the risk of a much worse outcome.

Sometimes when Jesus would go into towns, his reputation as a healer and meal-giver preceded him, and he'd be elbow-to-elbow with swarms of people crying out for his attention. Think Walmart on Black Friday.

As Jesus walked down the road in this chaos of people, he stopped, turned, and looked up at Zacchaeus in a sycamore tree straddling the branches. Selfish, evil, hated Zacchaeus.

Jesus looked at him and knew more than his name. He knew his potential. He knew his future. He knew his worth. In that very moment, the Son of God decided a meal with the town scum mattered more than what the religious leaders thought of him.

I don't believe he just happened to notice Zacchaeus by chance. I believe he sought him out. Jesus deliberately went to where he was.

There is a really crazy part of this story that is so easy to miss: Jesus invited himself over to Zacchaeus' house. "Hey, I just met you, and this is crazy, for I'm going to your house today." That takes some chutzpah, as most people don't like to be inconvenienced by strangers.

The other day, some guy I didn't know came up to me and asked me if he could borrow my cell phone. I looked around and tried to find some other person who would help, but no one was there, so I reluctantly let him use it. Then I went home and used three Lysol wipes on it.

But here Jesus just invites himself on in. I always try to read the social cues when I'm at someone's house, because usually people only have so much they can take of company. I could only ever invite myself over to a few people's houses. That is something only close friends get to do.

Only close friends. And Jesus invited himself to Zacchaeus' house.

Some of my new friends at the valet had been on my Facebook page and found out I wrote comedy songs. I did a Christmas parody of "Party in the U.S.A." by Miley Cyrus called "Party in Bethlehem" at a church Christmas party, and my valet friends saw the video on YouTube. They loved it.

They knew I was a Christian and went to church. I didn't hide it. And by that time, I had helped some of my other friends from church get jobs with us. We were slowly taking over the valet. We were the guys who shouldn't have been in Gainesville anymore, but for some reason still were. We had student loan debt creeping up on us, so we worked at the hospital valet. The other valet employees knew we were religious. My friends Brandon and Ryan would bring their Bibles and keep them on the podium they worked at every day as cashiers.

One day I was driving a car back to the parking lot and my new friend Steven came up to my car. I rolled down the window and he put his hands on the door, leaned down, and asked me out of nowhere, "Why are there so many Christian religions?"

I paused, and then looked back at him and asked, "Do you mean, 'Why are there so many denominations of Christians?'"

He said, "Yeah, that's what I meant."

Without hesitation, I said, "That sounds like a great question for dinner. We should grab some together soon." And then I drove off. That's also the same method I used when I'd ask girls to dinner. I'd just drive off before they could answer me.

Throughout the next month I tried to make plans with Steven. When we had the same shifts, I'd bring up getting dinner in the middle of goofing off.

"You free this Tuesday or Thursday?"

"Ah, no, sorry man. This week's not good."

"No problem. Next week?"

After a few weeks of failed attempts, we finally found a night that worked and I picked him up at his apartment and headed to Moe's.

This was the first time Steven and I had hung out one-on-one, and it's always weird for guys when that happens. It can pretty much feel like a first date. You're nervous. You're not entirely sure what to talk about. You're worried it's going to be boring and awkward. And then you don't know if you should kiss them or not, or who leans in first. You know, guy stuff.

He'd forgotten his wallet, so I paid for dinner, and we sat down. I didn't know I was going to do be paying for the meal, and it didn't help the "Is this a *date*-date?" vibe we had going. Luckily, he was never short on words, so I poured some salsa on my burrito and started listening.

He started talking about what he was up to lately and how much our jobs sucked. Then, all on his own, he transitioned into talking about his past and upbringing. He had grown up in and around church for the most part with his family and was close to his old youth pastor at one point in time.

Again, people are much more open to conversation than you may realize if you don't start it off by looking them in the eyes and asking them if Jesus Christ is their personal Lord and Savior and if they renounce the evils of idolatry, gluttony, and voting Democrat.

He talked to me about what he believed about faith, what he'd lost in his faith, and what he wished he'd held onto. He wasn't thrilled with where he was in life, and he wasn't proud of his past. This meal we were sharing was the first time he'd talked about this sort of subject to anyone in years.

I listened to him talk through it and probed him with certain questions to understand better and find out more. When he had finished his story, I dipped a tortilla chip into my salsa cup and asked him, "Do you think you are in a place right now where you could come to God? Do you feel like he'd accept you?"

He looked down and thought about it. My burrito was gone while most of his was still sitting on the table. Without looking back up he said, "No, not really."

I almost jumped out of my seat as I told him, "That's just it! You can! You don't have to fix yourself first. God loves you just as you are right now." I continued, "I could be the worst person in the world. I could be a thief or a murderer, and my mom would still love me. She'd still want to come see me. She would love me simply because I am her son. And that is exactly how God feels about you. You're still his son. The door is always open."

We ended the dinner on that note, got some refills to go, and talked about other stuff while I drove him back home. I walked him to the door, kissed him goodnight, and told him I'd like him to meet my parents.

Just kidding. We shook hands and agreed we should grab a bite to eat again sometime.

Zacchaeus turned his life around on the spot while Jesus was at his house. He gave back all he had stolen from people, and then some. He said, "Look, Lord! Here and now I give half of my possessions to the poor, and if I have cheated anybody out of anything, I will pay back four times the amount."[2]

It was more than just a change of actions; Zacchaeus had a change of heart. When you feel loved, you feel accepted. When you are accepted, you feel secure.

Security is what we all long for in some way or another. I believe at our core, we're all a Zacchaeus waiting to be found. We put our hope in what we can steal and hold onto. But when we encounter love and acceptance, it changes us. It changes what we are willing to give, and it changes how we are willing to receive.

It's one thing to be accepted; it's another to be sought after. Jesus didn't just let Zacchaeus tag along with the crowd; he hunted him down.

Zacchaeus, the wee little, terrible man, was somehow important enough for the Son of God to risk his reputation over. He was loved enough to be called out by name. And he was so very much accepted that he who once was a lying thief became a generous giver.

Everything changed. He was saved because he knew Jesus was seeking him out.

> *Jesus said to him, "Today salvation has come to this house, because this man, too, is a son of Abraham. For the Son of Man came to seek and to save the lost."*
>
> *Luke 19:9*

One night I was out with some valet friends and Eric asked me to give him a ride home. Somehow we got talking about his past and how he had grown up in the church as well. He used to even sing in the choir.

We each shared stories, both funny and personal. We talked so long that we ended up parking in front of his house. Again, this would have been another great date situation to share with an actual girl, but at least I figured my parents would approve of Eric because he was polite and tall.

Steven came up in our conversation, and I said we'd grabbed dinner a few nights ago. Eric said, "Yeah, Steven had told me you had been asking him to go."

"Oh, really?"

"Yeah, he was actually pretty skeptical at first. He said, 'Why does Jon keep asking me to go to dinner? Is he going to preach to me or something? I don't want a sermon.'"

I had no clue this had been said prior to our little man-date, so it hit me with a sinking feeling in my gut. Much like a Moe's burrito will. I was nervous people had been talking about me and worried I had creeped everyone out. I was scared I had become that religious guy who people roll their eyes at when he walks by.

Eric continued, "I told him, 'No way. Jon's not like that, man. He probably just wants to hang out.'" That was a relief to hear.

I thanked Eric for being a great friend and sticking up for me and helping kill the weirdness and hesitation I didn't know was even there.

Then he told me something else I wasn't expecting. "Steven said that he had an awesome time at dinner. He said no one had ever told him the things you were telling him. He said he wanted to go again and that we all should actually grab a meal with you sometime."

Eric and I continued our conversation, and I feel that night took our friendship a lot deeper. Just sitting in his driveway, we talked about faith and life and fears and regrets and hope. Again, people are quite willing to talk when you let them and don't stare them in the eyes asking them what their views on the End Times are and if they think the Mark of the Beast will be an Apple product.

Months later most of my close friends had left the valet or were in the process of leaving. I like to think of it as our great deliverance or our very own exodus. Steven was back in his hometown in the panhandle of Florida, and I was getting ready to move up to D.C. in a few weeks at the end of summer.

I was hanging out with my roommates at my apartment when I got a call from Steven. We didn't ever talk on the phone, so I was a little surprised to get it.

I said, "Hey, it's good to hear from you! What's been going on?"

"I met up with my old youth pastor back here at home. It was really great."

He continued to tell me about how they had reconnected and about some other old friends he'd seen.

"I've been doing a lot of thinking, and I feel like God has been calling out to me. I think I'm hearing his voice, and I feel like I'm coming back to him now. It's different, and it feels familiar at the same time. But I know it's God."

I said, "That is so awesome to hear! I'm so glad you are telling me this and that you are finding hope again."

Steven said, "Yeah, man. I'm just looking at where I was and what got me here and where I'm going. And I think . . . I think God brought you to the valet to bring me back to him."

God brought me to the valet.

I hated it. I didn't want to be there, but he was seeking his children out there. He was seeking me out as well. I needed to be found again and find out how deep and wide the love of God was stretching across my world.

Our names are important. Our integrity is important. But who are we worried about losing our witness in front of? Jesus said, "It is not the healthy who need a doctor, it is the sick."[3] And if by sick he meant those who aren't in a relationship with him, then what is it worth to heal them?

Are souls worth our reputations?

It is not a license to sin or an excuse to be entangled by the things of the world, but it makes me question how much I should want the approval of judgmental religious people if Jesus didn't need their approval.

That challenges me. And it scares me.

It scares me because I want to be liked. If I'm honest, I want to be esteemed and looked up to. But those are only accolades for my pride.

What does it mean to be a follower of Jesus? We are told some will despise us. I have always assumed many people in the world may not want to be my best friend, but it could be true of many inside the walls of the church, too.

The apostle Paul described the redemption of mankind Jesus gave us on the cross by saying, "God made him who had no sin to be sin for us, so that in him we might become the righteousness of God."[4]

Jesus was willing to bear the shame of the world, and in doing so, he became the hope of the world.

What does it mean to be like Jesus? Who did Jesus eat with? Who did Jesus seek out?

Consider where you are right now in your life. What are you surrounded by every day? Who are you surrounded by? Are you in your own version of the hospital valet, a place you don't really want to be?

I wonder if God has you there for a reason.

Maybe the reason shares a cubicle with you. Maybe the reason is on your bus route. Maybe the reason doesn't know your name yet.

What if we all were a Zacchaeus? Maybe we still are.

Hey, what have you thought of the book so far?

If you like it, please go write a review on Amazon! It'll really help.

Maybe you're thinking, "Is this guy really asking us to compliment him?"

No, I'm just asking you to be my wingman. Help a brother out.

If you have not liked the book then just throw it off a bridge and maybe some kids will find it like in *Jumanji*.

Chapter 8

Church in a Bar

How Jesus and John the Baptist Were Complete Opposites and Completely Alike

"I believe that we are here for each other, not against each other. Everything comes from an understanding that you are a gift in my life—whoever you are, whatever our differences."

John Denver

Have you heard the one about a Christian, a Hindu and an agnostic who walk into a bar? They start talking about sports, girls, life, politics, God, and of course, burritos.

They become friends. They hang out all the time. The Hindu and the agnostic become two of the Christian's groomsmen.

That isn't a very funny joke. It's what happened to me, though.

I clearly didn't grow up with any alcohol in my house. After all, we were terrified of Chili's. We eventually overcame our fears and developed a clear conscience about bar-and-grills, but I still had my guard up against alcohol.

I remember being at a Chili's one time with my parents when I was in high school. My dad ordered an O'Doul's non-alcoholic beer. I couldn't believe it was sitting on our table. It was the only time I had seen anything close to alcohol anywhere near my family. Also, here's something you'll never hear, "A round of O'Doul's for my friends!"

No wine for my family either. Not even on holidays. We basically crossed out the mentions of wine in the Bible and replaced it with "water and food coloring." It made singing some worship songs a lot harder, though.

> *Like oil upon your feet,*
> *Like Kool-Aid for you to drink...*

The closest contact I had ever had with wine was when I was in 6th grade. We were at my Greek grandfather Papou's funeral. We were in the basement of the Greek Orthodox Church and spread out at the tables were little shots of wine. I wasn't sure what it was at first. I thought it was salad dressing.

My sister and I were sitting by ourselves and dared each other to drink one, so we did. We thought it was awful. Maybe it was crappy wine, or maybe you're not supposed to shoot back wine like a Jägerbomb. Either way, it further confirmed my suspicion of the evils of alcohol. Though after sitting through an entire Greek Orthodox service, you can kind of understand why people would immediately want a drink.

Like I mentioned, in high school and well into college, I stayed away from alcohol. This may have come from a partially good place in my heart, but it was driven by fear. Actually, my first beer was with some friends I met through a Christian campus organization. I was hanging out with some guys at a house after finishing Bible study, and I was offered a Newcastle. We would have a beer or two around the house or occasionally at an Irish pub downtown called Durty Nelly's.

I found out Christians could drink beer and not be alcoholics, and I found out you can have many great conversations while sitting on barstools. I could enjoy a drink and not become demon possessed. It may sound silly to you, but this was actually a big revelation for me, and a new freedom. So parents, there you go—let your kids get involved in Christian clubs, and they will start drinking.

Let me pause to clarify my message. My point is not to defend alcohol or to judge anyone who doesn't drink. If you don't drink, I'm glad you don't. I have some great friends who don't, and we still hang out all the time. I think it's sad when people need alcohol to have a good time, because they are too boring and uptight to have any fun without it. Alcohol doesn't need another advocate, and I'm not trying to be one.

Some people say if we're going to criticize excessive drinking, then we should also come down on stuff like excessive eating, too. However, while gluttony is an issue worth addressing, no one has ever slept with someone they wish they wouldn't have after a night of consuming excessive amounts of ice cream. I haven't heard of anyone driving off the road, because they had eaten too much at a Golden Corral. Although, I've definitely felt like I was going to die after eating there.

Far too many issues and pain have been a result of alcohol, and my goal in this chapter is not to push it on anyone, or to make it seem cooler than it is. And we all know some people who should probably stop drinking altogether. Like many other topics, Scriptures can be used to either advocate or condemn it. It's an endless debate and what you believe is what you believe. This is just my story.

By the time I graduated college, I was comfortable with going to Bible study and then to a bar afterward. I also found out happy hours with coworkers can really make for some good conversations.

Looking back, it's funny that I was terrified of bars, but they have ended up being a means of connecting with people I would have missed otherwise.

I used to lay in bed at night and wonder who my groomsmen would one day be. Girls, you're not the only ones who have thoughts about your wedding, though you're the only ones buying magazines about it. Men think about it, too. Mostly the wedding night. But sometimes we think about the actual wedding day.

I'd also wonder which of my friends would still be around by the time I was married if the rapture hadn't taken place by then. "Well, surely him, him, and him. Probably not him." Never once did I think I would have a groomsman who didn't go to church with me—not because they had a different faith than I did, but because I just didn't think I'd ever be close friends with someone outside of the church.

Years later, the agnostic guy and the Hindu guy were two of my groomsmen. I didn't meet them at church, but I count them as brothers. Their love for me doesn't have anything to do with how much I know about the Bible or how many mission trips

I've been on, though they may think those aspects of my life are good or commendable. They don't even care that I have three DC Talk albums memorized. They love me because we have a friendship of trust, respect, and loyalty.

These friendships began in bars. Some of the best conversations I've ever had about life and God have been in bars. After a few drinks, people were willing to open up about their lives. Many times I hadn't even started the conversation. They started it with me, because they knew I would listen.

I don't want to lead anyone to believe I go into bars only to preach, or that is what my end goal is. I don't stand on the tables and lead hymns. The truth is, I go into bars to be with friends and build community. I don't just go into bars and whip out the Bible and start preaching. That would be like going hunting in the woods and shooting aimlessly and hoping you hit a moose. You might get a random squirrel, but more than likely you'll scare everything away and probably just shoot a friend instead. Just ask Dick Cheney about it.

I'm not scared of bars anymore, because I don't think Jesus is.

God has given us each a voice of our own, and we don't need it to be like anyone else's. Sure, there are people we can learn from and even follow their methods, but we should be as authentic as God has made us to be. I kind of view God as the Keurig machine and we are the coffee grounds. He's the one pumping the water, or life, through us, but we each have our own unique flavor to mix into it.

John the Baptist did his own thing out in the wilderness and had taken the vow of the Nazarene. The vow of the Nazarene, or Nazarite, was a vow Jews could take voluntarily to separate themselves for the Lord. There were a few strict guidelines, like not drinking anything fermented or eating grapes or raisins. You were not allowed to be near a dead body of any person or animal. You also were not permitted to cut your hair during this time. (Remember Samson? He had taken the vow, too. We tend to believe Samson's strength was in his hair, but his strength was in the vow. When his hair was shaved off of him, his vow was broken, and he lost his superhuman strength.)

So John the Baptist had taken this vow and was living in the wilderness with long hair, not eating grapes or drinking wine. He also was pretty rough and ragged in general, because the Bible says he wore clothes made out of camel hair and ate locusts with honey. Not exactly the breakfast of choice for me.

> *Hey kids! Have you ever been eating honey and thought, "Gee, this could use some locusts"? Try Locust-Honey Crunch! It's packed with fiber and healthy stuff that mom's like, too. Locust-Honey Crunch from Kellogg's!*

John the Baptist was a radical prophet when Israel had not seen a prophet in ages. At the time, they were mostly hearing from Pharisees who were manipulating the Torah. John came and started calling people to true repentance and then baptizing them. People would come from all over the place to hear John speak and then get baptized. His call was to prepare the way for Jesus. Kind of like the opening act to get the crowd pumped. John the Baptist: the original hype man.

> *"Yo, yo, yo, all you Hebrews and Hewbrettes! Y'all ready to get this thing started? Say Shalom! I'm about to bring out my main man who's ready to drop some knowledge and mercy on you! He doesn't need a spotlight because he is the Light of the world! Make some noise for Jesuuuuuuus!"*

Jesus, however, was a little more presentable than John. He had obviously not taken the vow of the Nazarene because he drank wine and raised people from the dead.

> *[Jesus said] "For John the Baptist has come eating no bread and drinking no wine, and you say, 'He has a demon.' The Son of Man has come eating and drinking, and you say, 'Look at him! A glutton and a drunkard, a friend of tax collectors and sinners!' Yet wisdom is justified by all her children."*
>
> *Luke 7:33-34*

Jesus was saying, "Look, John isn't coming anywhere near wine or the homes of sinners, and you think he's a freak. I am drinking wine and mingling with everyday people, and you think all I do is get drunk. We really can't win with you people, huh?"

When it comes to your methods of evangelism, someone somewhere is always going to have a problem with something. You're not using enough Scripture. You're using too much Scripture. You're not addressing sin enough. You're not relevant enough. You're trying too hard to be relevant. (This could go on for pages and pages, but you get the idea.)

What if Twitter had been around during this time in the Bible?

> *Who does @JohnDaBaptiz think he is? Quit it with the freak show.*

> *It's clear that @SonofMan316 is a drunk. #OverIt #MakeIsraelGreatAgain*

> *Flipping tables? @SonofMan316 needs anger management and respect for authority like @Pharisee_Bro.*

@SonofMan316 I lost 35 pounds in a week on the Nazarite diet. Ask me how!

People will always have opinions. In fact, you can say that about any single action you ever take in your life. Someone will always have a different opinion. Some people will never like you, and there is nothing you can do about it. Tina Fey once said, "If you ever start to feel too good about yourself, they have this thing called the Internet, and you can find a lot of people there who don't like you."[1]

Some people are going to have a problem with this book. Hey, I have a problem with this book. So there. Beat you to it.

People are always going to want to voice their stupid, petty judgments about anything you do. But do it anyway.

I think the distinction between Jesus and John is so important when we look at the church today. Jesus never went to John and said, "Hey man, how about you start doing what I'm doing to reach people. Let's hit the pub."

And John never told Jesus, "Get out of the cities and the houses of sinners. Be more like me. Want some Locust-Honey Crunch? No? All right then, more for me."

During my time in Gainesville, I was still new to the bar scene. I was really enjoying being in a new atmosphere, especially one which I had avoided so heavily in the past.

I miss my Gainesville days, despite the struggles I had. I would go to the Friday night prayer service at the church for an hour or two and then head out and meet some friends at a bar in town. I remember one time leaving the prayer meeting and thinking,

"Am I really leaving church and heading to a bar?" I kept waiting to feel guilty, but I didn't. The *me* of a few years earlier would have rebuked myself and told me I was living a double life. But I really felt close to God and desired to be around the people God loves.

I remember one Friday night around 11:30 I was walking out of a bar near campus with some friends who had grown up in church as well and were going through their own overcorrecting experiences. We saw some people we knew from one of the Christian organizations on campus. They were standing outside with clipboards and pens. My friend Ryan, who I knew both from church and my valet job, came up and gave me a hug with his clipboard in hand. No matter where he was, everybody liked Ryan.

"What's up, man? Doing alright?"

"Yeah, great to see you."

They didn't have to say what they were out there doing; I knew just from looking at the clipboards. They were out evangelizing and asking people coming out of the bars to take a survey. One of those surveys asking them a series of questions that progressed into some deeper life thoughts. Thoughts on love, purpose, eternity, and God. I knew this because I'd done it before myself.

We chatted for a few seconds and then said goodbye to Ryan and his crew and walked on. One of my friends made an off-the-cuff comment on what they were out there doing, "Oh, that'll be really effective," as we kept walking. I didn't say anything. I understood where his comment was coming from, because we had both used those methods in the past in different places and hadn't seen a lot of real effectiveness come from it. Still, I remember thinking, *Good for them.* Just because the clipboard method didn't work for us, doesn't mean it doesn't work for other people. Maybe we were just really bad at it.

This moment has stayed near me all these years because I think it was a beautiful illustration showing what the church can be like, and not what the Internet comment sections have made it out to be. Ryan saw me coming out of the bar and never once chastised me for it. He never even questioned me on it. He never told me to come out of it, and I never told him to go into it. God was using him as he was with his own Keurig coffee flavor.

If someone doesn't feel comfortable going into a bar, why should they go? John the Baptist was effective where he was and how he was because God had called him. Ryan and his friends were effective where they were and how they were because God had called them.

I remember in high school there were goth kids. I'm not sure if they're still around these days or not. They were the ones with black fingernails wearing black JNCO Jeans and more bracelets than you can count. When I had to walk by them in the hall I would never make eye contact. Goth kids scared me. I was always afraid they'd hold me down and put purple eyeshadow on me.

The goths wanted to be rejected by society, yet they all hung out with each other. Even the people who don't want to be accepted by society actually want acceptance.

I believe in Gospel crusades, church plays, and street evangelists. I understand why people want Christian music on the radio and some televangelists on TV. I believe in high school mission trips to foreign countries. I've been a part of all of these ministries.

I believe they all have their places in the message of the Good News, but above all of them, I believe relationships are what really change people at their core. I've heard a lot of good sermons and songs, and some have really impacted my life. The most effective changes in my life, however, have come from my relationships. People who have invested in me. People I know and people who know me.

I suspect many people outside the church already know the gist of the message. They have access to sermons, seminars, and whatever the heck they're showing on TBN these days. People aren't short on information. What we desire is community.

Community is why I believe in the church. We can listen to a good sermon anywhere nowadays. We can download the best worship music planet Earth has to offer anytime we want it. But you cannot download people . . . yet.

People want to belong, no matter what they tell you. Have you ever met someone who isolates himself and thought, *Wow, what a nice guy*. You usually think, *That dude is creepy*. No man is an island, and if they are then they are likely miserable and talking to volleyballs.

Not only do we all want community, we need it. It is in our DNA the same way wolves run in packs, birds flock together, and girls all go to the bathroom at the same time.

My friend Dan is a Lieutenant in the U.S. Navy. (Yes, we've made plenty of *Forrest Gump* Lieutenant Dan jokes.) We were talking recently about the community he found and built during his deployment at sea. I'd like to say we were talking after a solid workout or sharing a breakfast together in the early hours of the morning, but the truth is we were playing Halo together online and talking over our headsets like eight-year-olds.

Dan said the community he made between the other officers was not only part of the experience, it was necessary. At least once each week, he would meet with a few other officers and basically have a group therapy session on the ship. Each officer would share their highs and lows of the week and get a chance to voice their frustrations. They were safe to do so, and it was vital to their mental stability while being away from everyone they loved. It was a way to handle such a unique, draining situation like being deployed at sea for months. Community was not just something they did when they were bored. Community was ingrained into the process and crucial to their mental survival.

Even if you do not believe in God, you have to admit humans share a common need to belong to each other. And when I look at humans as creations of God, I see us as beautifully designed creatures who were not only built to be connected to God, but built to be connected to others.

Not only connected, but dependent on each other.

> *For just as each of us has one body with many members, and these members do not all have the same function, so in Christ we, though many, form one body, and each member belongs to all the others.*

> *Romans 12:4-5*

If you talk to any ambitious college kid, you'll most likely hear of all the places they have traveled in their short lives and all the countries they still want to see. They hold their stamp-filled passports up in pride, like a banner of their life experiences in culture and coolness. Traveling is fun and exciting and gives you the opportunity to take in cultures you can never truly experience by watching documentaries. Some people build their lives around going all over the world as much as they can, and they have more souvenirs than you can count.

I've done a decent amount of traveling in my day, and I plan to do more of it. Yet, I don't think I have the travel bug so many of my peers and the younger generations seem to have. After a few days I start to miss the comforts of home, even things like free refills in restaurants. I wish I loved to travel as much as I love saying I love to travel.

I want to be cool and adventurous, but at my core, I think I'm just more of a homebody. Traveling for me is usually like exercising. It requires an exhaustive amount of output. I hit a point during it where I want to die, and then at the end I'm glad I did it. But I'm also glad it's over.

I want to see the pyramids of Egypt. I want to go to the Grand Canyon. I want to do one of those tubing groups through caves. But more than any of that, I want to be a regular at a restaurant. Like Fonzie status. I want to walk in and say, "The usual, Lou." And if I could walk over and bang the jukebox to play some CCR without paying, well, that would be the cherry on top.

I want to be friends with people solely based on the fact that I eat somewhere consistently. I haven't lived in Jacksonville long enough to have a relationship with an establishment yet, but I am not giving up on being a regular at Burrito Gallery.

Any time you go to a bar, you will probably see someone who has a relationship with all the bartenders and staff. He's kind of just *that guy* people know there. His tab is never closed out. I'm not sure if there is a term for these folks. Maybe *alcoholics*? I'll likely never be a regular at a bar, because I honestly don't like drinking that much, and also it's expensive. I'd rather spend my money on watermelon and tacos. I've also hit the age where I look at a beer and quickly run the numbers in my head, *Is this worth the calories? Could I eat ice cream later if I drink this?* I wish I were joking.

Bars, in a sense, are their own church. There are deacons, elders, and cranky people sitting in the back who think the music is too darn loud. It is a body of its own where people commune and break bread and wine. The bread in this sense is pretzel bites or chips and queso. It is a place where people come and find a place to belong and a place to meet new friends and hang out with old ones. The show *Cheers* was built entirely around this idea. And we all know the theme song. "Sometimes you wanna go where everybody knows your name. And they're always glad you came." The church experience for many people is going to a place where no one knows their name, and no one really cares if they are there or not.

I grew up watching *Cheers*, but I still had an idea in my head that bars were just places where sin runs rampant and everyone who goes is just a drunk. When I finally started going for myself, I found out they were just full of people looking for a church of their own. People were even willing to put weekly offerings into a tip jar.

True, there are many who abuse bars and alcohol, and abuse is never good. But you could say the same of the church. People in bars are full of sin. People in church are full of sin, but they just may not admit it so easily.

The church has tried so hard to distance itself from a culture that is strangely similar to its own. It just operates differently. In both churches and bars, people want to belong to a body. People are people wherever you go. Bars offer a quick solution to your problems: "Here, drink this and forget about your pain for a night." Some churches offer the same quick fixes as well. "Here, sing along with us and forget about your problems for a while." Both have little lasting effect on someone's soul and self-worth.

The Book of Proverbs says, "The purposes of a person's heart are deep waters."[2] We are beings designed with incredible depths within us, yet we waste our time trying to merely satisfy our surface. It's like putting a Band-Aid over a wound; you can't just keep covering it up and expect it to heal. We are designed to go deeper. We long for deeper connection than someone remembering our name or sharing a drink once a week watching a football game.

Some of the deepest conversations I've had started in bars with friends. The coolest part is I don't even have to try hard to start them up, they kind of just happen, or someone else starts a conversation with me.

> *"Jon, I've been reading your blogs about faith . . ."*

> *"Hey, you go to church, right?"*

> *"I need you to tell me what you actually think, because I don't really trust the advice of my friends. They'll just tell me to drink it off; I need to hear something more than that."*

People aren't short on information; what we desire is community. Community that goes deeper than the superficial.

Psalm 42:7 describes this need in all of us:

> *"Deep calls to deep,*
> *at the roar of your waterfalls;*
> *all your breakers and your waves*
> *have gone over me."*

The psalmist is speaking of the depth of the human soul calling out for love. The love of God was the only love deep enough to wash over him completely. The only love deep enough to satisfy his deepest longings.

I think it's interesting how the Great Commission Jesus challenged us with was not to go into the world and make converts. It was to go into the world and make disciples. A disciple is not created by a one-time encounter or a one-time sermon. Disciples are made from doing life together. Jesus produced twelve disciples by living with them, not by preaching to them.

People are looking for community everywhere. Jesus said, "Where two or three are gathered in my name, I am there with them."[3] If the church is an extension of Christ, and if he is omnipresent, then the church must be omnipresent as well. Where two or three are gathered, inside the walls of a First United Methodist Church or inside Poor Richard's Pub, the church exists.

The church is where humanity's need for community intersects with God's love for humanity. Church is not a location but rather an intersecting event.

We were made with deep waters. We are not as superficial as we let ourselves be. What have we been trying to satisfy on the surface that can only be filled by greater depths of love?

In 1998, even before the Internet really took off, America was overloaded with the Bill Clinton-Monica Lewinsky scandal. Everywhere you looked there was some comment or news article about it. It kept going and going. Some Republicans, like Newt Gingrich, were calling for his impeachment.

The Christian, right-wing, conservative, uptight-citizens-brigade was on it. He had disgraced his country, the office of the President, his family, and God. It was a time where fingers were pointed like never before.

Was Bill Clinton wrong? Absolutely. There are no excuses for affairs, whether someone is the President of the United States or a mechanic at Pep Boys. Still, behind all of it, there was a man who clearly needed a Savior. He needed to experience the love of God more than ever. Not to pardon him from consequences of his actions, but to change him from the inside out.

Billy Graham has offered counseling to Presidents for decades, beginning with President Truman all the way up to President Obama. Naturally, Billy had a relationship with President Clinton, and during this time of scandal, the two men would meet for counseling.

As you would expect, many religious people threw stones at Graham and told him not to meet with Clinton. They called him a hypocrite and someone who has lost touch with God. Sound sadly familiar? When it would have been easier for him to avoid the outrage or just ignore the scandal altogether, Billy took the persecution and continued in his ministry anyway.

In response to critics, Billy Graham summed up his decision with this statement. "It is the Holy Spirit's job to convict, God's job to judge, and my job to love."

Have we been spending too much time trying to do God's job? What is our job? These questions apply to every single moment of our lives, and are worth us asking ourselves daily. Where is God calling us to go? Who is he calling us to live our lives with? Are we wasting our time pointing fingers when God wants us to be joining hands?

If we have ever drastically underestimated anything from the Bible, it is the extent of the grace of God.

We sing about it, read about it, and even experience much of it. Still, we have not even begun to understand the depths of grace that was willing to be nailed to a cross.

We know of grace, but we cannot truly comprehend it in our simple, human minds. It is not our place to make the final judgments, and we really have no clue what may come of all of our earthly endeavors and actions.

I believe in the end, the extravagant grace of God is really going to surprise us, amaze us, and perhaps anger some uptight, religious people.

Chapter 9

The Exaggerated Battles
of American Christians
What is the Best Form of Protest?

"The Republican party is the party of nostalgia. It seeks to
return America to a simpler, more innocent and moral past
that never actually existed. The Democrats are utopians.
They seek to create an America so fair and non-judgmental
that life becomes an unbearable series of apologies."[1]

Jon Stewart

The Daily Show with Jon Stewart has won more Emmys than you
can fit into a room. From 2003-2012, *The Daily Show* was not
only nominated for the award, but won each year for
"Outstanding Variety, Music or Comedy Series." Ten years in a
row they dominated the category until 2013 when they were
finally beat out by *The Colbert Report*, which was a spin-off of
The Daily Show.

Jon Stewart became a figure who millions of people turned to for
some inkling of truth, despite the fact that he is a comedian. *The
Daily Show* could not exist, though, without the 24-hour news

networks of CNN, Fox News, and MSNBC. The majority of the show consists of pointing out political hypocrisy and the ridiculous statements made by the network anchors. They have built a behemoth comedy show off of news network commentators who argue and complain for a living.

One of the most important moments of Jon Stewart's career was when he appeared on a CNN show called *Crossfire* in 2004. It was a show featuring a loudmouthed Democrat sparring off against an obnoxious Republican over political and social issues in front of a live audience. It was basically like Thanksgiving dinner with your family.

Jon came on the show and they thought they'd have some laughs with him since he was a comedian, but instead they got an attack. Despite the fact that *The Daily Show* was largely dependent on the ridiculousness of cable news, Jon pleaded with them to stop what they were doing because it was hurting America.

Paul Begala, the Democrat host, remembers the event and the discussion he had with Jon afterwards:

> *"Stewart thought it was absurd to pretend every issue could be reduced to a forced choice between the right and the left. I thought that was a good point. Some issues have seven sides, but better to air two than none.*
>
> *Then he said we deliberately booked the show to provoke division. Guilty. A discussion of religion, for example, would feature a debate between, say, the Reverends Jerry Falwell and Al Sharpton, when the truth is most believers fall somewhere in between. His criticism stung because I agreed this was a major shortcoming of our program."*

A few months later *Crossfire* was canceled. Some say the decline started with Jon Stewart's memorable appearance.

Though *Crossfire* went off the air long ago, *The Daily Show* and others like it continue to thrive because our media has become less about fact finding and holding politicians to integrity, and more about who can shout the loudest. This is not just the culture of the media, it is now the culture of society, and even of the church.

Social media has given everyone a pulpit and a voice. We all know the old adage, "The squeaky wheel gets the grease," and it's true. Nowadays you could say, "The squeakiest wheels gets their own primetime shows on cable news." People aren't looking for facts, they are looking for the next matter to be outraged about. You pick a side to be on and then you spend your time being upset with the other side.

It's true of everyday people as well. We have blogs and Facebook posts catering to a one-sided audience which get more attention than rational thoughts trying to see both sides. People are preaching to their own specific choirs and the choirs are eating it up. You pick a side to be on and stick with the script.

It seems like we've come to believe the people who are really good at complaining are also people who have good ideas.

It's war.

I think we, as Christians, have a tendency to lock ourselves into our own closed off houses. You could even call it a "house of mirrors." In this house, we basically stand around and just stare at ourselves. We hang out with people who share our beliefs. People who think like us. Agree like us. Talk like us. People who read the same Francis Chan books.

Now occasionally, we'll disagree about predestination versus free will, or we'll argue about what a real worship song should sound like. But we all still believe in Jesus. We all know the church lingo. We all challenge each other, but we don't really *challenge* each other.

If you are wondering why there are so many battles in the church, I think it is the same reason kids crammed into the backseat of a car get into fights.

When I was a kid in the back of our Cordoba, we had approximately four square inches of space for my sister and I to share. So sure enough, we'd fight constantly back there. Over dumb stuff. Over whose shoestring was crossing over onto whose side. Over the fact that we were tired of having to sit next to each other. We'd fight just to pass the time because we were bored.

Conflicts in the church can work the same way.

I can't do it anymore. I can't spend another second arguing predestination versus free will. I can't argue about hymns, the TULIP doctrine, or the gifts of the Spirit any longer. I've wasted precious hours of my life going back and forth with other Christians debating stuff from the Bible. Egos shouting at other egos in search of affirmation in the worst ways possible. It never leads to any growth of character or beliefs, it just makes people angry. Denominational holy wars only lead to death of our spirit and sanity.

Honest, pure discussion is good. We need to dig deep into the Scriptures together and wrestle with the facets of our faith that we are still figuring out.

But the thing about debates, especially on the Internet, is no one walks away and says, "Wow, you really changed my mind." It's just a competition of "who can sit here and do this the longest."

Actually, it's probably more of a "whose life is so uneventful that they have the time to do this" competition.

No one is really a winner when we all look like losers with too much free time on our hands and too much pride to shut up and walk away.

I've always been impressed by the apostle Paul's ministry tactics. Probably the coolest place I've ever been in my life was Mars Hill in Athens, Greece. I got to stand where Paul himself stood. Mars Hill was the meeting place for the Areopagus Court. It was also a place where the most intellectual minds in Greece would come and discuss philosophy, religion, and law. I got to stand on the edge of the hill and yell, "I'm the king of the world!" just like Paul did.

Paul would go there and challenge the thinking of the intellectuals of the day. He would listen to them. He would present his case for Christ. He would go through their marketplaces. He would allow himself to be absorbed in their culture without losing himself in it.

Paul and the other apostles were immersed in their local cultures and weren't afraid of disagreements related to their faith. In fact, they were even thrown out of cities because of their radical beliefs. They were full of the Holy Spirit and not afraid of trolls on Facebook.

I'm not suggesting that anyone needs to abandon their church or small group and become a wandering evangelist with a GoFundMe page. However, I do think we all need to find a way to get outside of our house of mirrors and get into the culture around us. Think about where Jesus went. He would teach in the synagogue and then go mingle with people at Chipotle. He was on fishing boats with his disciples, and then he was having

135

dinner with tax collectors and prostitutes. He was immersing himself into both sides. It's like when a musician gets into acting but still does songs for their movies. Jesus was the original Will Smith. "Wild Wild West Bank."

I think a common misconception among intellectuals is that you can make yourself sound smarter by making others sound dumber. That's like beating a group of third graders in basketball. Sure, it's awesome to go Dikembe Mutombo on them, but you don't actually look nearly as cool as you feel. The dumber you make people look, the dumber it makes you look, because apparently you surround yourself with dumb people.

There is still a place for civil discussion. There are Mars Hills everywhere waiting for you to present your thoughts, ideas, and beliefs and listen to the thoughts, ideas, and beliefs of others.

Go to some new places. Get your feet dirty. Feel uncomfortable for a bit. Get your brain and heart working together. A faith that has not been tested should be slow to be trusted.

My dad was the pastor of a very small church for a few years when I was really young, so some of my earliest memories are of crawling under pews and being in church nurseries. Some kid bit me in a nursery one time, and I've never forgiven him for it. I remember eating the extra communion crackers (the forbidden food of the sanctuary) with Melissa when my parents weren't looking. We would make up games in the church parking lot to kill time while my dad talked to missionaries and church members for hours upon hours upon hours. He may still be out there talking.

It always baffles me when I have friends who have never been to a funeral. I've been to so many I can't even begin to count. I've been to a whole lot of weddings, too. It was just part of growing up in church with a family who was super involved. The church is a place of weddings and new lives beginning, and it's also a place of funerals. It seems both life and death can be found in the church on any given day.

I remember being in kids' choirs and plays. Even back then I never had a main part, just some wussy solo in a song. Meanwhile, Psalty the Singing Songbook was sucking up all the glory.

I remember, as a six-year-old, kneeling by the couch with my family and praying that Bill Clinton wouldn't be elected. Apparently Hillary was praying harder than we were.

I also remember visiting people in trailer parks and how scared I was of the random dogs running around. I remember people arguing with my dad outside of our small church, because he wouldn't give them everything they wanted financially. Instead, he would offer them opportunities to do some work around the church. I remember visiting sick and dying people in hospitals and nursing homes, as well as, handing out food to people in need. And I particularly remember standing along the side of the road throughout my hometown with hundreds of other people from churches across the city holding up signs on one Sunday every year. Signs that read, *Abortion Kills Children* and *Adoption: The Loving Option.*

Interestingly enough, I don't remember ever having a choice to be a part of any of these things. My parents never asked me if I wanted to go. I just went. It's what we did as a church. As the people of God. I figured this was how we made God happy.

Once I hit my twenties, I started to rethink some of these experiences. I don't think the church is what I grew up believing it was. The church's four walls are not the holiest place in the city, the people within the walls are not always nice and loving, and the sermons aren't always 100 percent accurate.

I don't think Jesus was a Republican, and I don't think God is happy when we just put checks next to Republican candidates on the ballot with no thought whatsoever as to what their actual stances are on a variety of issues. Every day, I feel more annoyed with what people say the church should be and what people say a Christian should look like. Just because someone has a national show doesn't mean their voice is anything worth respecting. In fact, they constantly show me exactly what I don't want to look like as a Christian or even as an American.

I once read that President Obama was leading a war on coal. Really? Was he sending soldiers into the mines or something? I also heard that there is a war on Christmas. And I think I heard that there is a war on marriage, too.

Everything is a war these days. If I was "War" I'd be pretty offended that you were throwing my name around like that. "Hey, I'm War. I'm completely awful. Don't you lump this other stuff in with WWII. That's disrespectful to my past. I leave people dead and homeless, not just opinionated and annoyed."

Thanks to 24-hour news networks, everything has to be a big deal. Never forget that CNN, Fox News, and MSNBC are competing with *The Bachelor* and *Monday Night Football.* They want ratings just as bad as NBC, but they have to be reporting news all the time (at least what they call news). Everything has to be a war or no one will watch it. And when everyone is at war, no one is at peace.

Disaster and fear boost ratings. It's proven. Growing up in Florida, the only time we watched The Weather Channel was if there was a hurricane coming. We were glued to the coverage. Something about that Doppler radar just sucks you in. The same concept is what these news networks use. Disaster and fear. You had better hear what they have to say or you might lose your job or your civil liberties and everything you love. Nothing ever plays out to the extreme they say it will, yet we keep watching and listening to the rhetoric they have to throw at us. And they know it.

Can we admit we are in an age of extremes? Why does everything have to be so far one way or the other? Go read through your Facebook newsfeed or a YouTube comment section; I guarantee you'll find 99 extremists to every one peacemaker. I believe this is why Jesus said, "Blessed are the peacemakers," because he knew they are as rare as an actual good sale at Banana Republic.

We might like singing "Give Peace a Chance," but few people are willing to do what it takes to bring peace. Peace means compromise. We like the thought of "peace on my terms." Agree with my views, and we can get along. That's not real peace, but it's actually what we want, isn't it?

As a Christian, I am often annoyed with what I hear coming out of the mouths of fellow believers. Every time there is an election, it's like they finally open up the book of Revelation and start pulling random verses out and make them apply to various different aspects of candidates.

> *"And I stood upon the sand of the sea, and saw a beast rise up out of the sea, having seven heads and ten horns."*[3]

> *That's Obama! He came from Hawaii, which is in the sea! Seven heads and ten horns? Sasha and Malia are seven and ten years old! It all connects, don't you see? Wake up!*

Of course it goes beyond election season. Christians somewhere are usually boycotting something, like Disney. Then we get really mad when other people want to boycott the things we love, and we act like they are ridiculous for thinking a boycott could possibly work. We call it persecution. If that sounds like a double standard, it's because it is.

When I hear people make statements like, "We need to get America back to where it was," it makes me wonder what point in time they are talking about. Back to what?

Back to segregation?

Back to slavery?

Back to The Great Depression?

Back to Civil War?

Back to before Netflix?

What time could we possibly want to get back to?

Oh, maybe they mean, "Back to when it was easier to be a Christian, white guy. Back when we weren't challenged by anything. Back when Presidents and generals praised our religious beliefs. Back when we could say one thing and do another and there was no one to hold us accountable for our hypocrisy."

Now, obviously there are tragedies and heartbreaks every single day. There are issues worth getting upset about and taking a stand over. There is still endless room for improvement. I will say I am sad to see God being pushed out of agendas. I am sad to hear that people don't want to be a nation under God or be open to prayer. But most of my sadness comes not from God being moved out of the government and society, but out of our hearts.

I'd love it if Jesus was the President of the United States, but he's not. I don't know if he'd want to be, though. But since he isn't President, we are left with human beings running the show. The world would be at peace if we didn't have any humans, so if you really want world peace then maybe you should start praying for a plague. Until everyone on Earth dies out, though, you can bet Christians will continue to see things play out in ways they do not want them to.

I don't say that to be a downer, I say it because I am referencing Jesus.

> *"If the world hates you, keep in mind that it hated me first. If you belonged to the world, it would love you as its own. As it is, you do not belong to the world, but I have chosen you out of the world. That is why the world hates you."*
>
> *John 15:18-19*

So should we be surprised by disagreements with our faith? Should we be surprised when people don't want to celebrate Christmas with us? I mean, Jesus kind of spelled it out for us, didn't he?

So, what if there actually is a "War on Christmas"? What should our response be? Does God want us to flip out and spread more fear and outrage over Starbucks' red cups? Is that what brings change? Do we want to have everyone feel sorry for us? Or do we want to be stand-up people who aren't afraid of disagreement? People who can say, "I know whom I have believed and am persuaded that he is able to keep that which I've committed unto him against that day"?[4]

Mike Huckabee was on another one of his presidential campaign trails in 2015 during Indiana's Religious Freedom Restoration Act ordeal. He chastised liberals and the LGBTQ community and said, "[Their agenda] won't stop until there are no more churches, until there are no more people who are spreading the Gospel." He was essentially saying, "If you don't elect me, Christianity is doomed." If he is really the Christian he claims to be, then he I think he needs to read his Bible before he spreads fear.

> *"Therefore, since we are receiving a kingdom that cannot be shaken, let us be thankful, and so worship God acceptably with reverence and awe, for our God is a consuming fire."*
>
> *Hebrews 12:28*

I'm not even talking about civil rights here. I'm talking about using fear to get votes and saying Christianity will die out if we don't elect the right people. It's just not biblical. These politicians know exactly what they're selling, because it works. But just because it works doesn't mean it's right.

This woe-is-me Christian mentality needs to stop. Even if the government took away every church building, they could never take away the church. All over the world where Christianity is outlawed, the church is growing.

We cannot claim to be given a "Kingdom that cannot be shaken" and then say one elected official will take away everything we hold in faith. If one man can destroy what we believe with all of our hearts, then we have no hope at all. We are selling empty promises. If we think a government can keep the Kingdom of God from coming, then we must not really believe what we say we do about the power of God.

The Gospel doesn't need a government.

Jesus never ran for office, and he's never legislated himself into anyone's heart.

Sometimes I get so annoyed with the church. Then, I have to remember two things: I am the church, and she is the bride of Christ. So I had better not abandon her.

I don't think Christians need to shut up and just grin and bear it all. If anything, I want to echo Proverbs 31:9, "Open your mouth, judge righteously, and plead the cause of the poor and needy." Or to quote Malala Yousafzai, "I raise my voice not so that I can shout, but so those without a voice can be heard."

I've been wondering for some time now what the best form of protest is. Is it holding signs on the side of a street? Is it writing congressmen or marching on Washington? Maybe there's some good in those ideas, and maybe God has called some of us to do them. But maybe the steps towards the change we want to see in this world don't come with national headlines. Maybe change doesn't come by arguing with strangers in comment sections.

I've been thinking about when Jesus was talking to Pilate before he was crucified. He told Pilate, "Everyone who is for me is on the side of truth." Pilate responds, "What is truth?"[5]

I feel like Pilate in a lot of ways. I know I am on the side of Jesus, so I must be on the side of truth. But if I can be honest, sometimes the lines seem to blur due to all the noise, charts, and graphics on TV and computer screens. I'm left frequently asking, "What is truth?" But I think it is a question God doesn't mind us asking him.

The truth about truth is that whether it makes us happy or not, whether we can agree with it or not, or whether we want to accept it or not, does not change the fact that it is truth. While we are in pursuit of the truth, God may reveal some things to us we really don't like, or answers which might mean we have to eat some of our words.

What if the best form of protest is different than the ways we've advocated for change in the past? What if we were not just hearers and repeaters of the Word, but doers of the Word? What if we were people who kept our cool in the thick of the changes we didn't like?

The apostle Peter gave us some governmental advice and wrote, "Fear God; honor the king."[6]

He didn't say to fear the king; he said to fear God. Perhaps we are wasting our time getting up in arms about things that wouldn't be such a big deal if we learned what it truly meant to fear God.

The best form of protest is to live a holy life. To learn how to disagree in love and respect. To learn how to stand for truth first and foremost in our own lives. To hold ourselves accountable before we hold anyone else accountable.

I've always been impressed by the way Jesus handled his crucifixion. It was the most incorrect and unjust governmental and societal action in the history of time. A perfect man forced to carry his cross and die. But he took it with dignity and in holiness.

> "He was oppressed and afflicted, yet he did not open his mouth; he was led like a lamb to the slaughter, and as a sheep before its shearers is silent, so he did not open his mouth."
>
> *Isaiah 53:7*

Surely there are times for us to speak up and let our voices be heard, but we must at least consider the way Jesus actually handled his opposition. He shut his mouth. He stood for something greater than what any man could take away. The head of the church knew when to speak and knew when to stand silent.

I believe in the church, and I believe in the church in my country. The reason I love the church is because I'm allowed to be a screw up. I'm allowed to be someone who constantly makes mistakes and gets it wrong. I'm allowed to still be a part of the body of Christ, and I am encouraged to even boast in my weaknesses. It's amazing.

If we serve a God who is willing to find the best in us and continues to work in us despite our shortcomings, we need to be people who do the same for others. People who are willing to change.

Chapter 10

Identity Crisis
Who does the Perfect Christian Looks Like?

"If you are always trying to be normal, you will never know
how amazing you can be."

Maya Angelou

I went on a Eurotour when I was in college the summer of my
first senior year. (Yes, I had two senior years. We had a good
football team, so I decided to take a victory lap.) So I took some
student loan money and traveled with some friends through
Vienna, London, Paris, Athens, Pisa, Florence, Venice, and Rome
for four weeks. It was awesome, and exhausting. And expensive.
I ate a whole lot of PB&Js.

If you ever get a chance to visit Europe, you'll wonder why
asking your waiter for ice has to be such a massive ordeal over
there. You'll also see some of the most beautiful cathedrals you
can imagine. They rise high above cities for what seems like
miles into the sky. Their sanctuaries are gigantic, and they
usually have intricate passageways and catacombs. The amount
of detail in them is mind-blowing.

They weren't exactly funded and built "PBS style," with generous donations from viewers like you. Hundreds of years ago when many of them were built, Christians weren't holding weekend marriage seminars or mega conferences with Louie Giglio. The Roman Catholic Church ran the show. As a result, the Christian faith, which is meant to free people from the restraints and regulations of Old Testament Law, became a whole new law of religious practices, customs, and commands. Many of these enormous cathedrals for God were built through guilt offerings from the citizens.

The Catholic priests would offer monetary offerings for sins. It would kind of work like this: (Please read the following with a 1940s New Jerseyan accent for a more dramatic effect.)

> *Michael shows up to church.*
>
> *Priest is all like, "Hey, Mikey, how terrible have you been lately?"*
>
> *Michael says, "I told Joey Carmaggio he was a good blacksmith, but I was lying. Dat guy stinks."*
>
> *Priest says, "Ah, Mikey, that's messed up. Put some money in the jar over here unless you wanna be sleepin' with da fishes for all eternity.*
>
> *. . . Fuhgedaboudit!"*
>
> *[Insert more offensive, cultural stereotypes.]*
>
> *End scene.*

The more sins people supposedly committed, the better it was for the priests, because they could just guilt people into paying up. People would pay to receive indulgences for sins, to obtain special blessings on their lives, and to save their dead relatives from trouble in the afterlife. They were pretty much buying their way into the religion.

Cathedrals were built off of the guilt and manipulation of many desperate people, often ones who couldn't even read the Bible for themselves. They trusted the spiritual authorities who abused the faith.

Guilt is a powerful motivator and quite a useful tool if you want to manipulate people into action. Mothers and fathers use it on a daily basis because their mothers and fathers used it on them. It's a repeated practice because it works. Guilt may change someone's actions, but it never changes someone's heart. Guilt only works to the benefit of the one inflicting it. No matter how good you are, guilt never says that you're good enough or you've done enough.

Religion can be a lot like a cathedral. You stand in the middle of its magnitude. You feel small. Maybe even frightened. Your guilt builds up the walls, and you are swallowed up by the breadth and weight of the force surrounding you. Guilt walls us in from leaving the rules.

A religion that binds you to it out of fear is fearful itself. A religion that forbids you from asking questions is not secure enough in itself to be challenged. A religion that has nothing more to offer than "shall nots" and "do nots" is dead under the weight of guilt and burdens.

Jesus Christ came to give abundant life.

Jesus Christ sets people free.

Martin Luther, the original, not King, Jr., was a German priest back in the 1500s who is most credited with sparking the Protestant Reformation. The Protestant Reformation was the movement that took Christianity out from under the weight of the Roman Catholic Church, who was building all of those cathedrals. Martin Luther stood up against the practices of the church, like unnecessary indulgences, and ended up being excommunicated by the Pope.

One of the reasons this was such a big deal was because Martin Luther wasn't just some guy who rode into town out of the shadows—he was a priest himself. He had been under the weight of guilt, and he had been putting others under that same weight.

He was a man living under guilt and trying to exterminate it however he could by his actions. He even participated in a practice known as flagellation, which is when people would bring physical pain on themselves to atone for their sins. People would whip, flog, and even cut their bodies.

> Note: Flagellation is not to be confused with "flag elation," which is when someone is super excited about flags.

Legend says that Martin Luther received a revelation from God one day while he was trying to atone for his sins while crawling up steps known as the Scala Sancta, or "Holy Stairs," on his knees. It was assumed Jesus walked these steps after he had gone before Pilate prior to his crucifixion,[1] so if anyone else climbed the steps they would receive a one-year indulgence for each step. While Luther was on his knees trying to earn his way to God and settle the unrest in his soul, he claimed he heard the voice of the Lord say, *The just shall live by faith.*[2]

At once, Martin Luther realized he had been going about it all wrong. You can't earn a free gift. Indulgences aren't necessary if God loves us as we are. His life was changed forever upon this revelation, and he went on to write "Disputation on the Power and Efficacy of Indulgences," also known as "The 95 Theses," which was a list of questions and propositions for the Catholic Church. It is also believed he nailed the theses right to the door of the All Saints' Church in Wittenberg.

His newfound freedom in Christ also resulted in him being freed from the burdens of the Catholic Church. And then they kicked him out.

Apparently, they didn't like people messing up their doors. I understand that. I hate when I get door-hanger advertisements for lawn care services, so I can only imagine my outrage coming home to 95 confrontational notes nailed to my front door. At least use Post-It Notes, bro.

Even centuries after the Protestant Reformation, we still find ourselves trying to earn the love of Christ. Much of it may stem as a result from our parental issues and maybe never being good enough for our mothers and fathers. Never being effective enough for our bosses. Never being smart enough for society. All of these situations warp and pull on our view of God without us usually realizing it.

We work towards affirmation with our hands instead of our hearts. Guilt keeps many out of church by feeling like they are not ready to come back to Christ. And guilt keeps many walled inside of the church by feeling like they have not done enough. Our good works end up working against us, because we will never do enough good works to earn our way to God. It's a deception and a manipulation of freedom.

The Bible talks about how priests would make sacrifices year after year for sins, but those sacrifices could never fully wipe away sins once and for all. When Jesus died on the cross, he disrupted the cycle of giving sacrifices for sins:

> *"We have been made holy through the sacrifice of the body of Jesus Christ once for all . . . For by one*

sacrifice he has made perfect forever those who are being made holy."

Hebrews 10:14

His sacrifice was the ultimate sacrifice. When we move towards God out of guilt, we start to nullify the work Jesus already did. When guilt is what motivates us to move, it only moves us to more guilt.

Jesus Christ sets people free.

Holiness is a result of salvation. Salvation is not a result of holiness.

Have you ever heard the term *legalism*? If you've been in the church for more than five minutes you probably have. Church folks are terrified of being legalistic. People accuse others all the time of being legalistic. It's our version of Joseph McCarthy and the Communism Red Scare. People around the church like to out other people as legalists if they think they are one.

It's basically a fancy way of finger-pointing.

Legalism says you do what you do out of guilt or fear and not out of genuine love for God and love for people, like adhering to a set of supposed biblical rules.

"Oh, he's legalistic. He reads his Bible every day because he thinks he has to."

"She gives 10 percent of her income to the church because she's legalistic."

You get the idea.

Without a doubt, there is a lot of legalism in the modern church. It's all over the place. It's in my own life. On the other hand, I believe some churchgoers may call out legalism where it's not actually in effect.

We have people all throughout the church trying to create a formula of what it means to truly be a Christian. Some people are too legalistic. Some people don't adhere to the guidelines enough. Everyone seems to have an idea of what the ideal Christian looks like.

So who is the perfect example of a Christian? Billy Graham? John Piper? Bob the Tomato? Sometimes I wonder if Jesus himself would have been Christlike enough for some evangelicals.

I'd love to see a show called *Undercover Jesus* where Jesus joins a church in disguise. Jesus shows up to church one Sunday in his VW Bus and starts interacting with the congregation. Things would probably get really weird really fast. Especially if John the Baptist showed up for a few episodes smelling funky and eating Locust-Honey Crunch. There would, no doubt, be leadership meetings on how to handle the newcomers who were creeping out the regulars and the largest donors. The uptight religious would point to Scriptures and misquote them to Jesus' face. Maybe he'd turn over their Christian merchandise tables and coffee shops. The worship leaders would come running out in their skinny jeans super mad that he knocked their new worship albums off the rack. I'd love to see their reactions.

CBS, call me. We can make this happen.

"Undercover Jesus, *beginning this September. The Second Coming just went unnoticed.*"

As I expressed earlier, I get annoyed with politics. It seems like it is just bad writing. It's the same story over and over. Controversial, terrible scandals. Fake apologies. Two-faced agendas. Constant manipulation by the media and the pandering to the big financial donors and corporations. It's like we're watching the same reruns over and over, and no one will get up and change the channel. It is especially annoying during a presidential election season when you live in a swing state. You can't watch a video on YouTube without seeing an attack ad first.

The two major political parties usually have an ideal candidate. It doesn't matter how you started out and what views you may have held at one point in time. If you become a lead candidate for the presidency, you are forced to become who your party says you should be. It's true on both sides. They both have an ideal candidate.

I heard someone say they would have voted for John McCain 2008 if he had been who he is now during his campaign back then. But I don't think he was allowed to be his true self during the campaign. You can start off as a maverick (or an Iceman or a Goose) and say whatever you want about your past and how you rolled, but when it comes to being a Republican or Democratic nominee for President, you had better fall in line with the prepackaged ideals and statements. Whenever you hear complaints of some candidate flip-flopping, it's accurate because they all flip-flop.

Members of the political parties want to hear you regurgitate back to them what they expect to hear. They don't want to hear anything different. As a result of this, every election ends up being between the same two people every single time.[3] They are packaged differently. They even sound different at first and full of new hope, but at the core of it all, it becomes the same two candidates every election. The same rhetoric and sound bites again and again.

I highly doubt that what we hear pitched at us in debates, public appearances, and statements is the complete truth of what a candidate actually believes. How many more failed marriages and sex scandals do we need to hear about until we realize that so many politicians don't care about families the way they say they do.

The same practice abounds in the church. When people come under the impression they are what a Christian should look like, they try to make other people look like them as well, instead of helping them become more like Jesus. We produce our version of the ideal Christian.

"*This* is the music a Christian likes. *These* are the people Christians hang out with. *This* is the candidate a Christian votes for. *These* are the issues a Christian stands for. Kirk Cameron is a wonderful person."

So does being a Christian mean you have to fit into the mold the church has created for all Christians? I don't think so. Bearing the name of Christ surely means things won't be the same as they once were, but you should not become just another paper doll. I believe God made us all unique for a reason.

Unity doesn't mean we are all identical. Jesus called us to make disciples, not clones.

The people who have helped me grow the most have been the ones who encouraged me in my strengths and differences. They didn't try to make me like them. They saw who God made me to be and was making me to be and did what they could to be a part of the process. And as a result, I inherited many of their qualities while expanding on my own.

Over a decade ago, a guy named Scott decided not only to be my friend, but to make an investment into my life. He's not only become my partner in many different projects and ministries, but also the guy I go to for advice. The reason I go to Scott is not only because I trust him and admire his life, but it's because I believe he really is on my team and wants what is best for me. I believe this because he made an investment into my life, and as of today, I've earned him approximately $0, so he's not in it for the money.

You can get advice from anyone and anywhere these days, and people love to give it, many times without being asked for it. Or they will charge you for it. Very few people are willing to make investments, though.

At the time we met, Scott was running a Christian coffee house in Ocala called Cafe on the Rock, and for a few years, it was a thriving, active scene for local musicians. By the time I was about 16 or 17, I had been playing guitar and writing songs for a few years, and Scott had me playing at the cafe every month, sometimes multiple times a month. Just me and my guitar up there mostly. I'd improv with the crowd and make up songs about the people walking out during my set. I learned to think on my feet and be ahead of the joke. I wasn't a breakout star or anything, but Scott saw something in me and decided to invest more. He gave me the chance to learn and build my gifts.

Scott and I do not share many of the same skills. He doesn't really like public speaking or writing, but he's done whatever he can to allow me to have a voice. He's set me up with radio shows, TV shows, and music and comedy gigs. We've never made anything off of our projects other than a sympathy check here and there, but I'd hold the experiences and memories we've shared up to any amount of money. He's a constant sounding board for ideas and encouragement. And we both give each other a lot of LinkedIn endorsements, which are arguably the highest honor you can give someone.

That's how you make a disciple. It doesn't have to be *Tuesdays with Morrie*. It doesn't have to be like in *The Mask of Zorro* when Zorro wants to train a new Zorro, although it would probably benefit us all to do some push-ups over burning candles. Jesus found twelve men and just lived life with them. He challenged them. He listened to them. He ate and drank with them. He traveled with them. Jesus didn't just hand out advice—he made an investment.

Making disciples doesn't mean you have to come up with a year's worth of curriculum for your pupils to study. It doesn't mean lesson plans or that you have to have an office they meet you in every Wednesday afternoon. It especially doesn't have to start with an awkward conversation.

> *"Excuse me, but I would like to disciple you with my wisdom and experience. Light those candles and start doing push-ups over them. And I would prefer you to call me Sensei."*
>
> *"But I don't even know you—"*
>
> *"You will call me Sensei!"*

Making a disciple means you just do life with them. And as you start to invest, it just kind of happens.

So who does a perfect Christian look like?

You can say that perfect Christians look like Jesus. Cool, but *how* do they look like Jesus? Jesus was a vagabond preacher walking around with twelve men and occasionally rubbing mud in people's faces. Should all Christians be homeless, unshaven evangelists? Or should we uniquely display the love and practices of Christ while maintaining our unique, God-given qualities and strengths?

156

In 1 Corinthians 12, Paul used the analogy of the body of Christ again. He said everyone who loves Jesus is part of the body. Some of us are hands. Some are feet. Some are eyes. We each have a place. A foot shouldn't feel any less a part of the body because it's not a hand. In the same way, you shouldn't look at others and think they matter more than you do just because they are preaching on Sundays, and you are working in the nursery. Every part of the body matters. If you've ever stubbed your toe in the middle of the night, you know how much that toe matters when you feel that sharp, unexpected pain and scream so loudly the Stricklands can hear you from across the street.

I fear too many followers of Jesus are fearful to display their faith, because they feel they are not an accurate representation of what it means to be a Christian. They are scared to try and lead others, because they don't think they can. They feel they are too messed up, too broken from their pasts, or not smart enough.

I think the perfect example of a Christian is someone who is not perfect at all. Someone who has scars. Someone who doesn't have every part of their life put together. Someone who makes mistakes all the time.

Jesus told a story in Luke 14 about a man who was throwing a huge banquet. After all of the invites were sent, no one showed up. So the man said, "Go out quickly into the streets and alleys of the town and bring in the poor, the crippled, the blind and the lame . . . Go out to the roads and country lanes and compel them to come in, so that my house will be full."[4]

Do you know why I feel like I am the perfect example of a Christian? Because Jesus wants the ones no one else wants. He wants me even in my struggles with loneliness. He wants me when I feel worthless. He wants me when my job doesn't want me anymore. He wants me when I keep repeating the same mistakes. He wants me when I feel like no one else in this city wants me.

He wants me just because he loves me. Jesus wants the ones no one else wants.

There's a great feast going on and you have been invited. Bring your worn-out clothes. Bring your drug addict friends. Bring your divorce papers. Bring your fear. Bring your depression. Bring your pornography. Bring your minimum wage job. Bring your anger. Bring your past.

Jesus wants you. You're exactly who he's been waiting for.

Chapter 11

Full House Lied to Me
Why I Can't Run Away from Home

"Have you found Jesus yet, Gump?"
"I didn't know I was supposed to be looking for him, sir."[1]

Forrest Gump

If you've ever been to the Magic Kingdom at a Disney park (if you weren't boycotting Disney), you've probably been through Frontierland. Frontierland has Splash Mountain, Big Thunder Mountain Railroad, and even the Country Bear Jamboree you may have had to sit through with your parents at some point. One of the most overlooked spots in Frontierland is a place called Tom Sawyer Island. You have to get there by river raft to this day. Tom Sawyer Island has been a part of the Disney parks since the beginning, but it is so unvisited that many people just think it is part of the background scenery.

Cultured people would have read the books, but I remember watching Tom Sawyer and Huckleberry Finn movies when I was a kid and wanting to have the adventures like they had. Maybe with a little less racism involved, though. Something about getting lost in the woods, building a raft, floating down the

159

Mississippi River, and faking my own death sounded like so much fun. I wanted to have an adventure of my own.

I've noticed if you ask most guys what place they'd like to visit, they will probably say Australia. I think it's because Australia represents adventure to us, and there seems to be so many opportunities for it over there. We all want to take on the unknown with our Crocodile Dundee knives and run with the kangaroos.

Most of us dream of adventures, but much like Tom Sawyer Island, our adventures often go unvisited. Tom Sawyer Island can't compete with the animatronics of Splash Mountain and the food on the streets of Frontierland. Our dreams of adventure can't compete with our iPads and the comforts of home. So we live life knowing in the back of our minds our adventures are out there somewhere, but they're just not worth the effort right now. Maybe someday.

This doesn't mean we're not adventurous people, though. But as you age, you think things through a bit more. You're wiser. You're also more cynical. And probably most of all, you just have more to lose.

If you consider the characters in most stories who set off on a journey for adventure, they are usually young. Luke Skywalker was a young man. Jim Hawkins in *Treasure Island*, just a boy. The Brave Little Toaster, a little toaster who was brave.

If the story deals with full grown adults, they are usually thrust into adventure against their will, or at least not seeking it out. Like in *Interstellar, Gladiator,* or even *Up*.

Adventure doesn't have to mean jumping on the next ship for Australia or packing up the car and driving without a map. It can just mean trying something new. Trying out a softball league in your city. Learning to play an instrument. Waking up early to exercise and getting in shape. Joining a church. Showing up to events where you don't know anyone. Becoming a child mentor. Adventure can mean a wide range of different actions and activities.

It seems the natural order of life causes our dreams to become less and less imaginative the older we get. We're resistant of new ideas and changes, because it's just time consuming or tiring. Sometimes what was once our adventure eventually turns into our obligation. The exciting becomes exhausting.

And maybe we've been disappointed one too many times by our past attempts. It takes a lot of effort to keep an open mind. To stay optimistic. To try again. It's all so very tiring and reeks of pointlessness.

Yet, millions of people feel lost every day of their lives. They hate their job. They hate where they live. They hate what their existence has turned out to be. And they lose themselves in Netflix every night to distract themselves from their realities. Getting lost on an adventure is part of the excitement, but to be lost in a day-to-day life you're continually unsatisfied with is depressing.

We are people made for adventure and change, yet we've settled for what we know. Because what we know is safe.

There's no risk or rejection involved. It's comfortable even if it's not ideal.

If you read through the Bible, or talk to any Christian who has walked with God for a long time, you may pick up on a few consistent themes. One theme in particular is the journey into the wilderness.

For many people in the Bible, it was a literal wilderness. God had Abraham pack up and travel into an unknown land, without a map or a plan.[2] Jacob ran from Esau and slept on rocks.[3] Joseph was sold into slavery and taken throughout different lands far from his home.[4] Moses ran into the wilderness after he murdered a slave driver and found out people knew about it.[5] David ran for his life from King Saul for years.[6] Elijah hid in caves.[7] John the Baptist lived in the wilderness.[8] And one of the first recorded stories of Jesus is him being led by the Holy Spirit into the wilderness to be tempted by the devil.[9]

The wilderness is never painted as a joyful time of life. It is a place of struggle, loneliness, and frustration. When we enter it, we may think we are being punished by God, or we may think God has forgotten us. We may even think God is torturing us just for kicks. It's often hard to pick out a set reason for pain and trials, and there are many moments I don't think we'll ever get answers for in our lifetimes.

The wilderness seems to be a common, and necessary, part of our journey in life and faith. In the midst of its weight, it is also the place where people encounter God in a way they had not before.

Jacob wrestled with God and had his name changed to Israel. Moses met God at the burning bush and was called to lead his people out of slavery in a great exodus. Elijah was called out of the cave he was hiding in and stood closer to the glory of God than ever before. David wrote many of our favorite psalms during the years he was running for his life.

Not many people seek out the wilderness, but they are thrown into it nonetheless. And in what would seem to be the place to lose all faith, it turns out to be what strengthens our faith the most. It's not safe. It's not fun. But it somehow changes us for our good. It's a spiritual surgery.

One of my favorite people from the Old Testament is Gideon from the book of Judges. Gideon was an unlikely hero, and like many adventurous stories, he was kind of thrust into adventure against his will. I think he was also pretty forgetful, because he kept leaving his Bibles in hotel rooms.

God was looking for a leader to deliver the Israelites out of a seven-year oppression from the Midianites. They were the bullies in the lunchroom. For example, each year the Israelites would plant crops, and the Midianites would come in and destroy them all. As a result of all the bullying and torturing, a bunch of the Israelites started living in caves and holes in the ground. They hid themselves from their enemies and lived in constant fear.

One day an angel of the Lord came to Gideon and said, "The Lord is with you, mighty warrior."

Gideon replied, "If the Lord is with us, why is everything so bad right now? Why do we hear stories of God parting the Red Sea and delivering our ancestors from slavery in Egypt, but here we live in fear for our lives every day? Where is *that* God at? God has abandoned us."[10]

The angel said, "Go in the strength you have and save Israel out of Midian's hand. Am I not sending you?"

Gideon said, "Hold on. I am the most insignificant person in my family. And my family is the weakest out of all the families. I am literally the worst of the worst."

Gideon needed to get to a Tony Robbins conference ASAP. He got into a dispute with God. God kept saying, "You're the one I want for the job," and then Gideon made him prove it in a number of different ways. If anyone ever lacked faith in the Bible, it was Gideon.

Finally, though, he accepted his calling and God used Gideon to free his people from their oppressors in an incredible way. Gideon led an army of just 300 men into battle against an estimated 135,000 Midianites, and God gave them the victory. The Midianites were so afraid of his army that in their panic they started killing their own men. Gideon was thrown into adventure against his will and ended up saving the lives of thousands.

While Gideon was saving his people, God was saving Gideon.

At the beginning of this story, Gideon represents so many Christians who have grown up in church. We've been going to church so many years it has become just like any other part of our week. We like the stories we hear about Jesus, and we can quote them and even preach them. But we haven't seen God do anything in a long time, if ever, so we settle for the monotony of church and faith. Like Gideon, we ask, "Where is *that* God when we need him?"

We wait in expectation.

Then we wait in anxiety.

Then we just stop waiting.

It can sometimes even get to the point where new and excited believers annoy you. We think, *Yeah, you're excited now, but give it a little bit and you'll settle down.* Truthfully, there is some wisdom in that cynicism. There is also laziness in it as well, but I understand the frustration.

You are told you are worshiping a God who is able to do anything, but you see so very little difference. People get sick

FULL HOUSE LIED TO ME

and die without being healed. Marriages fall apart. People stay poor. At times I think it would be easier to be an atheist, because then you could explain the random chaos of life by not having to explain it. You could say that everything just happens, and you don't need to waste your time looking for a reason. As a Christian, it feels like we are required to say, "God is in control."

God is in control? What does that even mean?

How can we say that when everything seems so out of control? How can we say he is in control when prayers are going unanswered? How is God in control when our loved ones die? How is he the friend who sticks closer than a brother when we feel alone and lost?

As Gideon said, "If the Lord is with us, why has all this happened to us? Where are all his wonders our ancestors told us about?"12

Gideon doubted God to his face, but God didn't walk away. He chased Gideon.

In the church, there seems to be a common fear in many to bring up any questions or doubts about God. They are restricted areas. We fear expressing any anxiety or lack of faith, because many Christians treat it with contempt, as if the walls of the church can't handle any rattling questions. We get told doubt can wreck all the miracles of God or destroy his plan for us. When prayers go unanswered, people look around the room and try to figure out who the faithless Doubting Thomas is.

It's sad how Thomas, one of the twelve disciples, has forever been labeled "Doubting Thomas." The guy made one mistake, and no one ever let him forget it. Thank goodness I'm not labeled by my mistakes or I'd be called "What Was the Deal with the Sideburns Phase Jonathan." Or "Almost Burned His Fingers Off Making Mac and Cheese Jon." Or "Made Too Many Jokes at His Panera Bread Interview JT." Or . . . you know what? That's enough examples. So if what Thomas did was enough to staple a label like that to his name for all time, then most of us should have "Doubting" in front of our names, too. Or something worse.

People walk into a sanctuary every Sunday with their own doubts and reservations, yet they are scared to vocalize them for fear of being reprimanded or backed into a corner. I fully understand why a free-thinking, curious individual with some doubts would not feel welcome into atmospheres of some modern churches.

But God can handle the questions. People act like God is a college professor who doesn't know what he's talking about, and the nerds keep challenging him, so he kicks them out of class.

We shouldn't completely discredit the power of doubt, though. There were times when Jesus sent doubters out of the room when he healed someone.[13] I think it can definitely come into play in certain situations, but I think it's amazing how Jesus handled Thomas's doubts. He restored Thomas. He didn't smack him in the head. The church should be the place where people are free to say, "Hey, this doesn't make sense to me," and have honest discussions and wrestle through the issues together. These questions can never be settled if we are too afraid to share them.

Many of us have doubts at some point. I think it is natural. I don't run from mine anymore. I used to be afraid to question God. Now, I take my questions directly to him.

He can handle it. He still chases me.

Like most kids in my generation, I grew up watching *Full House*. It was one of the only shows my Greek grandparents liked to watch with us, because Uncle Jesse Katsopolis was Greek, too.

As a result, I wanted to start a band like Jesse & the Rippers, grow out my hair, and play Elvis cover songs.

The show also gave me a misperception of how family issues were resolved. If you go back and watch the episodes, any time one of the kids would get upset and run up to their room, at least one to four adults would quickly follow up after them. Seriously, watch any episode. They'd get down on one knee and have a heart-to-heart while some cheesy music kicked in. Within 90 seconds, all love and understanding would be restored, a lesson would be learned, and the credits would roll.

I came to find out it was total bull. I tried this method a few times at my house. "You don't get it, Dad!" I'd run to my room faking tears and sit on my bed staring at the door waiting for a gentle knock. I even had some cheesy background music cued up on my tape player.

No one ever came to my room. And after about 15 minutes of waiting, I'd come back out and watch *Night Court* with my family, because I hated being alone, and no one would say anything about it. My parents' just waited me out. It was the most pathetic stand-off of all time. Thanks, *Full House*.

I've never been able to run away from home. I'm too much of a wuss. I'll admit it. I remember when I was a kid, I got so mad at my mom and sister one day, I said to myself, "That's it! I'm running away from home, and then they'll be so upset when they realize I'm gone. I'll finally get some of the respect around here I deserve!" The youngest are always trying to gain some respect. It's why I identified with Kevin McCallister in *Home Alone* so much.

I packed up my backpack with some shirts and shorts, a pocket knife, and a few toys in case the nights were lonely. I walked out the front door without saying anything to anyone and started on my Tom Sawyer journey. Unfortunately, I didn't live anywhere near a river and had no clue how to make a raft anyway.

I remember turning the corner on our block and watching the house disappear. Never mind that I biked around these streets every single day and had gone three times as far before, this time it was different. I was on the lam, and there was no turning back, until I walked a few more streets and realized I was hungry and had no clue where I was actually heading. I was nervous. I decided these few minutes without me were probably enough for them to learn their lesson, so I turned the corner and headed home.

Surprisingly, my mom and sister had actually come looking for me. I remember Melissa sticking her head out of our massive, red Crown Victoria and yelling my name. *They're actually looking for me,* I thought to myself. My great joy was soon overcome by great fear when I realized they were upset, because I hadn't told anyone where I was going. After a nice berating by my mother (and Melissa who for some reason felt the need to get involved), I got sent to my room. No cheesy music-filled *Full House* visits followed.

I've never been able to run away from God either. I've tried, but I'm still just the angry kid who wants to be Tom Sawyer, goes halfway around the block, gets scared, and comes back with poison ivy.

When I was 26, I had been unemployed in D.C. for a while, doing temp jobs as I could find them. After quitting my valet job in Gainesville, I had moved from Florida to D.C. to live with my sister and brother-in-law, Nick, in hopes of finding better opportunities. For two years after graduation, I'd tried to get something off the ground but couldn't, so I moved in with my sister, which made me feel like I was the out-of-work slob brother-in-law living in the basement like you see in TV shows and movies.

With a bachelor's degree in advertising, and after moving to a major city, I still couldn't get a job to save my life. I couldn't even get hired at Best Buy or Panera Bread. I had tons of friends inside and outside of the church who were gainfully employed and getting married while I was single and lonely. Everything I had tried to pull off in any area of my life was not clicking. I had stayed as faithful as I could to God and stayed involved with church.

If you don't know, nothing kills your spirit quite like applying for jobs all-day, every day. Especially when you're either hearing "No, thanks," or nothing at all. It's an unmerciful kind of purgatory. When people say, "We'll keep your résumé on file," what they really mean is, "We've already forgotten about you."

One day I'd had enough. As you've read in previous chapters, I do have my breaking points and don't have a great track record of keeping it together on the outside when I'm not together on the inside. I had returned from another interview and was taking off my suit next to my bed. I kicked off my shoes and as I began to remove my tie, I felt that familiar bubbling over of emotions and pain. The kind that result in public meltdowns.

I screamed at God and cussed him out. With tears building up, but too angry to cry, I said, "You do not provide for those who are faithful to you! Where is this powerful God I believe in? You suck at your job. I wish I didn't believe in you, because it's worse knowing there is a God who is sitting there and watching me and not doing anything about it!" I am censoring out the expletives, so this book won't be banned from Christian bookstores.

I wish I could say it was the only time anything like that happened, but it's just not true. Each time I was really angry with God in my past, it would usually play out like this: I'd tell God he's too hard to work with, too hard to follow, and that he didn't care about my life, because if he did then things would have looked different. I'd say, "I'm done. Come find me if you want." Then go to a bar with some friends, have a couple of pints, and by the fourth or fifth one I was usually in tears confessing my stupidity to them while saying, "I know God loves me, and I'm sorry. I don't want to run away." Ah, there's nothing like crying in front of your friends in a bar.

I've found God doesn't scare so easily. He's not threatened by threats. He uses my parents' technique of just waiting me out. And while it can come off as unsympathetic, it's anything but. If you've never cussed God out, then you are way better than me. I certainly have given him much more than a piece of my mind.

After I had screamed and cussed God out, I fell across my bed and buried my head in my pillow. I knew I wasn't alone, and I began to cry.

I've found that when the dust settles and my rage dies out, I have felt a gentle peace flood into the room. It doesn't mean my problems are fixed or that the pain immediately evaporates, but I know I am not alone. It's as if we stand face to face with God and punch him and push him and rail against him while he stands there silently. And once we have exhausted ourselves, we collapse into his everlasting arms. That's when he just holds us.

He can take it. He's not scared off by anger. He's patient when we are impatient. He's gentle when we are violent. He's calm when we are filled with rage.

The beauty of Jesus is that he chooses to come sit in the dirt with us. And in the moments we most feel alone and scared, he is with us. That's why Jesus is also called Emmanuel, which means "God with us."

He never runs away. He runs after us.

One night while I was still living with Melissa and Nick, both of them were out traveling for work. It was a hot and humid September evening around 10 p.m., and as I was winding down for bed, I heard the sound every person from Florida knows and lives in constant fear of—the sound of the air conditioner dying.

I went to the unit and couldn't see an issue. I checked the fuse. Nothing I knew to do was working to fix it. I thought I had broken it, so I had no choice but to call a repairman in the middle of the night. I was told it would cost around $300 for him to come out and fix it. I was unemployed and running out of money every day. But I had him come, nonetheless, because it needed to be fixed.

At an hour before midnight, the guy didn't show up skipping and singing to say the least. He looked like a linebacker, and I had apparently called him away from the bar. Clearly annoyed, he asked me what the problem was. I explained as best I could, which for me was, "Um, it stopped blowing cold air." I continued with my knowledgeable input, "It was blowing cold air, and now it's not blowing cold air . . . It's hot air now." I tried to have an awkward conversation with him, because I don't do well with silence. But his answers were short and uninterested.

He removed the panel from the A/C unit, and we discovered a huge block of ice had frozen onto the side. Apparently, this sort of thing happens when you constantly run the air. It was a problem that had likely been brewing for weeks. His suggestion was to get a hair dryer and use it to melt the ice. Still in fear for my life, I ran and got one. Also in fear, I offered to do it myself.

I stood there blow-drying a chunk of ice as he sat on a step by the front door. I asked him if he wanted a beer, then went and got us two. As the ice began to melt, so did the tension between the two of us.

I continued to ask him questions, and he finally started to answer me. He started laughing at some of my jokes and commentary. He asked me questions, like what I was doing alone in a house that size. I used to lie and tell people it was my house and then see how long it would take them to find the wedding pictures on the wall of a bride and groom without me in them. It usually didn't take long for them to figure out I was the little brother.

The night progressed. He'd been there for an hour or so, and the ice finally melted. He had to go check the unit outside, so I went out with him to hold the flashlight and continue talking.

He stooped down to the A/C unit next to some bushes in the backyard and began telling me about how he had a young daughter he was losing touch with. He shared his daughter with a woman he was not married to, or even in a relationship with anymore. He told me how it had fallen apart, how he wanted to be a better father, and how he wanted to fix his life.

I stepped a little closer to give better lighting. I asked him if he believed in God, and he said he did. But he felt he was not in a place where he was anywhere close to God anymore. His mistakes and regrets stood in between them. Instead of being angry with God, though, he felt guilty and responsible for the outcome of his life. Kind of like the way it feels when you are driving and run out of gas—you know it's your fault, but there's nothing you can do about it now.

I stood there holding the flashlight in the humid backyard and listened to a man pour out his heart to a stranger he'd only just met. A man who had walked in the front door annoyed and silent, but a man who was filled with pain and remorse. A man whom God had been chasing.

I told him about mistakes in my life, my regrets, and my messed up relationships with family and friends. I told him about my meltdowns. I told him how I had expected more for my life than living unemployed at my sister's house at 26 and that I had doubts about God. How I questioned why he would not only allow pain in our lives, but at many times, seemed to lead us right into the pain. I told him I didn't understand it, but I had hope.

Hope that we are not alone in the journey. Hope that we will eventually make it out alive. Hope in restoration. Hope in mercy. Hope in a greater purpose beyond fixing A/C units at midnight, or even beyond being unemployed.

God was chasing both of us that night.

He looked up at me, one hand holding a screwdriver and the other wiping the sweat from his forehead and said, "Man, I think you might be an angel God sent to me."

I looked him square in the eyes and replied, "Do angels get discounts?"

"Nope."

He gave me the receipt for the bill, took my credit card info down, and we shook hands. I told him I'd be praying for him and his daughter. I gave him my number if he ever wanted to grab a drink and talk sometime. And at 1:00 a.m., I finally went to bed with cool air running through the house again.

In the days that followed, I kept looking for the bill to show up on my credit card. I looked in the mail dreading its arrival. But it never came. Still to this day I sometimes wait for it to show up out of nowhere.

I guess sometimes angels do get discounts.

My wife and I don't have any kids yet, and I am the baby of the family. So my experience around babies is very limited. I think they are cute and all, but I get bored with other people's babies. Babies don't understand my political commentary or care to hear all the fun facts I know about Beatles' songs. They kind of just sit there and make people take care of their every little need. Babies are so selfish.

It must be hard at times to be a parent and be so unappreciated. Your entire life changes. You are consumed with taking care of a living, breathing human being, and you don't ever get thanked. A baby is completely helpless, but will never remember who cleaned them, fed them, and kept them safe.

I think we're all bigger babies than we acknowledge. God is constantly watching over us in unnoticeable and unappreciated ways. We're busy. We're angry. We're trying to fix the problem ourselves. We want a better answer than the one we're given. It's easy to get lost in the wilderness and lose sight of God, but just because we cannot see him does not mean he stops watching over us. Chasing us. Keeping us. Saving us in ways we'll never recognize or remember.

Recently, I was driving through Tennessee during autumn. It was a beautiful time to be in the Volunteer State. The leaves were changing, the skies were blue, and it wasn't freezing cold. I love the mountains and the big chunks of rock you get to drive right by. I understand why people live there.

We don't have mountains in Florida, so I was doing my best to take in the beautiful scenery while staying on the road at the same time. It's hard to do. You have to use your peripheral vision and maybe get a glance or two every now and then. You're seeing these beautiful sights one quick look at a time.

It seems the older I get, the more my faith in God changes. It's not like I love him any less, or I even believe him any less, but my faith isn't identical to what it was twenty years ago. Or ten years ago. Or even one year ago.

When I was a kid, I knew God was big, and he loved me. I knew the Bible had an answer for every question life could throw at us. The biggest question I had was why God wasn't healing me on the spot when I would get a cold. I honestly cherish those early years of my life and my faith.

My faith has since evolved from children's church answers to something that is now strong enough to battle my doubts and failures. My faith still remains, but my views on God can't exactly be given as an elevator pitch anymore. Our relationship is detailed.

Still, I keep searching for God, and as I search for him, he keeps finding me. It's a beautiful game of hide-and-seek we play. Sometimes he counts, and I hide. Sometimes he hides, and I count. But somehow in each game, we find each other. Even when I think he's found way too good of a hiding place sometimes.

For me, I think faith in God is a lot like driving through Tennessee and trying to take in the sights. You can't completely take it all in. You see outlines and maybe a couple of shapes and colors. You get a beautiful glimpse of a glorious sight far off, but you couldn't explain what you just saw in detail. Still, you know it's beautifully intricate and magnificent.

Paul described this view in 1 Corinthians 13 and said, "For now we see only a reflection as in a mirror; then we shall see face to face."[14]

We will never be able to fully put our eyes on the wholeness of God in this life. We'd be annihilated. The Bible says Moses got to see merely the back of God, and his face was shining so radiantly afterward that he put a veil over his face.[15] The glory and the complexity of God is too much for a human mind and body to take in. For now, we only get to have one or two second drive-by glances. One day we'll see it all clearly. Face to face.

Whether we seek out adventure or are thrown into the wilderness unwillingly, God is chasing us through it all. He's chasing us when we feel him so close in overflowing joy, and he's chasing us when we can't find him, can't feel him, or can't get an answer.

Does God confuse you?

Me, too.

Do you read the Bible and put it down and say, "What the heck did I just read?"

Me, too.

And it's all right. God isn't asking us to completely understand him. He's inviting us to love him. He's rounding up the neighborhood for an awesome game of hide-and-seek. Come join the search.

It's exciting. It's complicated. It's faith.

Chapter 12

God Did It
How I Deal with Atheists, Science, and Questions

"Rabbit's clever," said Pooh thoughtfully.
"Yes," said Piglet, "Rabbit's clever."
"And he has Brain."
"Yes," said Piglet, "Rabbit has Brain."
There was a long silence.
"I suppose," said Pooh, "that that's why he never understands anything."[1]

The House at Pooh Corner

When I was about eight years old, I was shown a puzzle. It was a simple box with perpendicular lines running through it. The objective was to draw one continuous line through each section without overlapping your line and without going through a section twice. The guy showing it to the group of us kids said it took him thirty years to figure it out. We all jumped at the chance to solve it much quicker. I didn't solve it that night, though.

For the next twenty years it was my go-to activity when I was bored. I'd draw it on the back of offering envelopes during sermons. I'd attempt to solve it during hundreds of hours of school lectures or waiting at the airport. It was this lingering challenge from my childhood that I was determined to figure out.

After thousands of attempts, I finally broke down and went to the Internet for help. I felt so defeated and ashamed as I asked Google for the answer. My shame quickly subsided and turned to anger. It turns out, this particular puzzle, which had plagued my mind for decades, was unsolvable. It is mathematically impossible to beat it. What kind of sick person would give kids an unsolvable puzzle?

I spent so many hours of my life pursuing an answer I would never receive. For some reason, I couldn't let the puzzle go.

The trouble with the wilderness, and life in general, are the questions. We're people who want a good story wrapped up like it is a 30-minute sitcom. We don't do well with lingering ideas or inconclusive evidence. We like the idea of closure, but life and the universe are open-ended systems.

In 2010, I went with a group of friends to see *Inception* when it was in theaters. Christopher Nolan is a genius, and everything he does is amazing.[2] I remember at the end of the movie when the top kept spinning and then the credits rolled. My friend Dan looked at us all and said, "All right, we're going to say the top fell over for my sanity's sake." I agreed.

The first *Serial* podcast had everyone glued to its investigation of such an interesting story. Any time you walk through a Starbucks you can still hear people discussing it. Each person with their own conclusions on whether or not Adnan Syed was actually guilty. I've never heard anyone say, "I guess we'll never know." Same with *Making a Murderer* on Netflix. I got sucked into that one. So many theories are flying around the Internet right now. We don't do well with questions.

It's normal, though. We love mysteries and the unknown, but we usually need a conclusion. And if one is not provided, we'll decide our own.

Look at comment sections all over the Internet. Those people don't like asking questions; they only like making statements. Nobody ever comments, "Please, tell me more about your idea." They only write out comments like they are absolute, indisputable truths.

Sometimes the trouble with faith is the lack of answers for what it requires us to believe. I have a number of atheist friends whose lack of belief in God doesn't come from not liking Jesus. They think Jesus was a good guy. They just cannot get past the lingering questions—unanswered scientific gaps Christians fill in with "God did it."

Where did Earth come from? God did it.

Where did the genetic code from? God did it.

An agnostic friend once told me the reason he had given up on his path towards becoming a youth pastor, and even just walking with God in general, was, "Questions led to questions that led to more questions. I got tired of never having an answer." It's in our DNA to want answers. We hate living with questions. We hate unsolvable line puzzles. And the Christian faith is full of its own gaps.

It drives scientific minds crazy. It's feels like a cheap cop-out. Like at the end of a movie when "it was all just a dream" or "aliens did it." It's like we approach these complex ideas and mysteries and can't come up with anything better, so we say, "God did it." Or, "Well, that's why you have to have faith."

I don't think we have to just accept the questions either. Part of what annoys atheists about Christians is when we give up on pursuing answers. Neil deGrasse Tyson, world-renowned astrophysicist, said he didn't mind people having faith so much as he disapproved of their faith keeping them from pursuing knowledge. He doesn't approve of the "God of the gaps" being the be-all and end-all.[3] I don't think I do either.

I've been an atheist a few times in my life.

One time, I was an atheist when I was a kid. I did some serious soul-searching and concluded there must be no God if I can't ever see him, and he won't play Nintendo with me. My period of enlightenment lasted about 12 minutes and then I really wanted our family to go to Pizza Hut, so I started praying again.

I was an off-and-on atheist when I couldn't get a decent job out of college. As I said before, those moments would usually last for a few hours until I was crying into my beer at night.

I was an atheist when I was watching *Cosmos* with Neil deGrasse Tyson. That series has some stunning information. *The universe has been around how many billion years? That's where dogs came from? That's it. I'm an atheist.* Then a few minutes later I thought, *Wait, what about stuff like purpose, love, the afterlife, and being cognizant of my own existence? Okay, I'm a Christian again.*

The truth is, I'm probably not smart enough to be an atheist. Most atheists I know are bright people. They read a lot. They know what words like *anthropomorphic* mean. They study the ins-and-outs of scientific theories and philosophies. I, however, can tell you the names of everyone who worked at Dunder Mifflin.

I have to say, I understand where atheists are coming from, especially with the loud-mouthed, facts-avoiding, right-winged media hogs making it harder on the God followers. Still, I really hate how there has become what seems to be only two major sides to choose from:

You can be an extremely liberal, atheist Democrat, or you can be an ultra-conservative, gun-toting Republican. You can be a complete cynic of any spiritual possibility, or you can be an unquestioning believer who will accept any explanation just as long as you attach Jesus or Ronald Reagan to it.

There must be more options somewhere in between. I'm realizing I'll never be PC enough for some liberals. I'll never be Christian enough for some conservatives. So I should probably stop trying to make both sides happy.

There are scientific views which don't conflict with the Bible that some conservatives still stand their ground against, like the earth being 6,000 years old. Why does the earth have to be 6,000 years old to prove God's existence or for the Bible to be accurate? I think when Christians choose their battles poorly and stand in defiance over some issues we just make ourselves look silly.

John Lennox, a brilliant mathematician and philosopher of science, said:

> "As both a scientist and a Christian, I would say that [Stephen] Hawking's claim is misguided. He asks us to choose between God and the laws of physics, as if they were necessarily in mutual conflict . . . For me, as a Christian believer, the beauty of the scientific laws only reinforces my faith in an intelligent, divine creative force at work."[4]

I don't see why God and science have to be at war with each other. Can't God be big enough to set into motion scientific theories and events? Can't scientific evidence be inconclusive enough to be open to an explanation involving a higher power?

Still, the lines have been drawn. People feel pressured to choose between science and God. I don't get into debates anymore with atheists, especially not on the Internet. I don't believe anyone ever really argued anyone else into the Kingdom of God.

Jesus never said, "Go ye into all the world and outsmart everyone." I think it's why Jesus intentionally picked out people who weren't the brightest scholars to be his disciples.

> *Brothers and sisters, think of what you were when you were called. Not many of you were wise by human standards; not many were influential; not many were of noble birth. But God chose the foolish things of the world to shame the wise; God chose the weak things of the world to shame the strong.*
>
> *1 Corinthians 1:26-27*

Atheists don't like Christianity because of the unanswered questions. But I've never done well with atheism, because I think we still end up with many of the same questions. We just have different answers for them.

When you stop and think about it, we all believe something that sounds insane.

I believe a universe was created by a timeless, omnipotent, omnipresent, loving God. He had one begotten Son who came to earth in human form to die for the people he created, and he never sinned. Jesus dying on the cross makes me free because of his blood that was shed. He is coming back, but his Spirit is with us now. We're waiting for him to burst through the skies and return for his followers.

I get it. It sounds insane. It's hard to swallow and process, and there are a billion items in between the lines that I honestly still have no explanation for.

But what is the alternative to faith in God?

An atheist usually believes the entire universe, with all its intricacies, physical laws, and mind-blowing sights, all started with a burst of energy. The Big Bang all of a sudden happened in one massive burst of energy. That's where the sun and stars and galaxies came from. It ignited a process of evolution for billions of years to come. Even our bodies, full of white blood cells, a central nervous system, capable of feeling emotions, came as a result of this bang. We exist and we are self-aware enough to even question our existence and experience love. Even if the Big Bang happened, what happened before it?

We all have views that hit a breaking point where there is no explanation. When you hit those breaking points, it all can sound a little insane. We may never be able to erase the word *why* from our vocabulary.

I'm learning all the time. This chapter isn't meant to be me trying to outsmart anyone who is an actual genius. I barely passed biology in high school. Thousands of scientists could beat me any day on *Jeopardy*. I just think it's absurd to say that we have definitive proof God doesn't exist and that anyone who believes in a God is stupid. I don't like when atheists talk down to me because of my faith.

Carl Sagan was a well-known astronomer, astrophysicist, cosmologist, and a million other titles of words I can't pronounce. He had a life full of scientific discoveries, accomplishments, and awards. He wasn't exactly a church deacon, but he wasn't certain science could explain everything either. Look what he said in 1981:

> *"An atheist is someone who is certain that God does not exist, someone who has compelling evidence against the existence of God. I know of no such compelling evidence. Because God can be relegated*

to remote times and places and to ultimate causes, we would have to know a great deal more about the universe than we do now to be sure that no such God exists. To be certain of the existence of God and to be certain of the nonexistence of God seem to me to be the confident extremes in a subject so riddled with doubt and uncertainty as to inspire very little confidence indeed."[5]

When I was a kid, one of my favorite movies was *The Rocketeer*. We recorded it on VHS back when Disney would do those free Disney Channel weekends. (My mom was so proud of herself for figuring out how to work that VCR. It was like she had discovered penicillin.) I wanted to be the Rocketeer and fly off into the clouds with my jetpack. I didn't really know who the Nazis were, but I wanted to fight them, too. I watched it all the time.

I recently rewatched *The Rocketeer* and couldn't believe some of the flying sequences. It looked so fake and cartoonish. You could clearly tell it was just a guy in front of a green screen flapping around. I was kind of heartbroken, because up to that point, that movie was planted in my mind as being so realistic. And in its time, I'm sure it was realistic in comparison to others, because we didn't have the special effects like we have today. But held up to what they are doing with movies now, it just doesn't cut it anymore. What once was breathtaking has become kind of cheesy.

Some Christians build their faith around ideas they have been told for years. If you come against their ideologies with any scientific evidence, they will not only refuse to do any research of their own, but they'll reject it right from the start based on their preconceived ideas. People look dumb when they have beliefs, but they don't know why they have them. It looks especially dumb to those who pursue scientific formulas and conclusive evidence.

When we firmly hold to the ideas of ages past as science and culture progresses forward, we make a dead religion out of a living and active Scripture. We hold to the nostalgia of a previous generation's religion. Like *The Rocketeer,* we remember it differently while the world has been progressing.

Jesus constantly called out the Pharisees for killing a living text by making the Torah so concrete. They got mad at Jesus for healing people on the Sabbath Day because the Hebrew law said not to do any work on the Sabbath. They tried to constrain a text, and hold people to those constraints, when the Living Word was standing right in front of them. Their beliefs were meant to evolve into faith in Christ. They held so firmly to their customs and practices that they missed the very Messiah they were saying would come.

Some people outside the church think many Christian ideals are holding up a progressing culture by using petty arguments based on random verses of the Bible. It's hard to imagine any religion progressing, and it's difficult to understand what it should even look like. You don't want to throw out the foundational beliefs and doctrine, yet we have to expose the parts that have been added to it over the years. In Christianity's case, what has the church added on?

At one point in time, American churches were fine with slaves sitting in the back of the church, or even their wealthy members owning slaves. They manipulated random verses of the Bible to justify it all. These became beliefs based around a culture and not beliefs based on Jesus.

What if Christianity was strong enough to evolve and not lose its truth?

Jesus addressed the evolution of faith:

> *"No one sews a patch of unshrunk cloth on an old garment, for the patch will pull away from the garment, making the tear worse. Neither do people pour new wine into old wineskins. If they do, the skins will burst; the wine will run out, and the wineskins will be ruined. No, they pour new wine into new wineskins, and both are preserved."*[6]

Religion built on rules, customs, and old practices we just keep repeating over and over is a brittle religion.

Religion held together by nostalgia will crumble when culture changes and new questions arise.

Christians lose faith in Christ when their religion can't handle new scientific evidence. They lose faith when their beliefs are like old wineskins cracking under new pressure.

When people hear music by Elvis Presley, they immediately recognize it. It's easily distinguishable and still loved by millions worldwide today. He is clearly still the "King of Rock and Roll," but if a new artist came out today singing with Elvis's iconic voice and style, we'd all say, "This is stupid." People still buy Elvis's albums to hear Elvis sing his music, but culture has progressed, and people don't sing like Elvis anymore. You stick out like a sore thumb if you imitate Elvis in any way, and people think you belong in Las Vegas. We like our nostalgia to be set in place, not to be reworked.

The Word of God is living and active and not really similar to Elvis. The Gospel is able to evolve with the times. Not only is it able to, it is meant to. The foundation doesn't change, but the stiff rules and ordinances we set into place will evolve or will break off if they are just based on a cultural ideal or trend. The question is figuring out what should continue. And that's a question we'll never be done with, but in which, God gives us grace and guidance.

And the truth is, Christians will never agree completely on doctrine. We have a ton of denominations built around one religion. Christian denominations divide over difference in doctrine such as:

- *Predestination or freewill*
- *Is Jesus coming back before the Tribulation or after it?*
- *Do miraculous gifts of the Holy Spirit still happen today?*
- *Should you use any instruments in church services?*
- *Should women be pastors?*
- *Should we pray to the saints and Mary?*
- *Is Joe Flacco an elite quarterback?*
- *Can we tell our kids about Santa Claus?*

Those are just some of the differences in doctrine that divide the church all over the world. It sounds insane to people outside of the church that we can't even agree on doctrine, and yet, we all say we follow the same Jesus. We all read the same Bible, but there are an estimated 30,000 to 40,000 Christian denominations. To be fair, many of the denominations are separate organizations, not separate beliefs, but still—over 30,000? I feel like someone held their finger down on the 0 key too long when they listed the stat. So I get it. It sounds insane.

However, I don't think it makes us weak. If your faith is in old wineskins, it may make you weak, but the message of Jesus isn't fragile. It can handle disagreements and differences. We are diversely designed people, but we can be united. Diversity doesn't have to prevent unity.

Unity doesn't mean looking identical. We're never going to look the same, and if we did it'd be way too freaky. Unity is not the same as uniformity. Some of my best friends are people I disagree with on a number of issues and ideologies, but we love each other and don't have to agree. It doesn't really matter unless you want to be right all the time. And if you want to be right all the time, you probably don't have many friends. You're the guy at the party who walks in and people roll their eyes. Stop being that guy. Stop spending your life in a comment section.

On the night Jesus was arrested, he gave his disciples a command:

> *"A new command I give you: Love one another. As I have loved you, so you must love one another. By this everyone will know that you are my disciples, if you love one another."*

> *John 13:34-35*

That's it. Love each other.

Love.

Jesus didn't say, "Everyone will know you're my disciples by your rules." Or, "They'll know you are my disciples by your secret club handshake. Get it down. And it'd better look cool, guys." He didn't even say, "Everyone will know you are my disciples by your doctrine."

I don't mean to diminish doctrine. It's highly important. And I don't think we need to rip ourselves away from our past completely. There is a lot of good woven throughout the church's history, though many refuse to see it.

But the command for followers of Christ is not to be right about everything. It is not to outsmart the unbelievers. It is not to have an answer for every challenge brought forward.

The command is to love.

God is not science. God is not answers. God is not theology. God is not doctrine.

God is love.

The love of God is like a new wineskin. It endures. It can handle a diverse culture. It can handle questions.

I wish the Bible had a Q & A section in the back with Jesus where he could go through and give a clear-cut, indisputable answer to every subject we could ever come across. But we don't have that. What we have is a God who leaves us with questions.

I have many experiences that seem like random experiences. I have many trials I can't connect to improvements in my life or character. I see suffering and inexplicable injustice all over the world. The more I look around, the more unanswered questions I gather every single day. Questions lead to questions that lead to more questions. I am coming to realize some of these questions may never be answered in this lifetime.

The main question I come face-to-face with every day is this: Can I serve a God who leaves me with questions?

Can I love a Creator who keeps me wondering? Can I trust in his goodness? Can I trust in his system of judgment?

It's easy to sit in the United States and argue the existence of a God. We have books. We have the Internet. We have food in our bellies. We have time to sit around and read blogs and arguments. But many do not have these luxuries. And many are not looking for scholarly expertise and well-crafted opinions.

They are looking for action.

Can I believe God is just when I see injustice? Can I believe in a God who does not answer all of my questions?

I think I can.

When I get past all of the questions, doubts, and opinions, I find what I'm truly looking for is not merely answers. I am looking for hope.

God doesn't give me all the answers I want. Instead, he offers me hope. With hope, I can move forward. With hope, I can love. And with love, I can act.

Since when does love make complete sense? We still don't understand it. Millions of books have been written and are yet to be written about love. We love our wives and husbands, and we don't understand it. We love our children when they have angered us beyond belief, and we don't understand it.

I understand about two percent of all of this, but I believe it. Maybe that's all that faith is. Maybe honest faith that God approves of can only say at times, "I don't understand this, but I trust   you."

Do we trust God enough to be wrong? Do we trust he is bigger than our errors and changing views?

If we believe in Jesus then we believe God loved us enough to come to us as Emmanuel. We serve a God who wants to be known way more than we even want to know him. If you seek him, he will find you, because he's looking for you, too.

I think I'm okay with "I don't know." I don't have to have answers; I just need love.

I'm not really into modern art. I've been to the Museum of Modern Art in NYC, and the National Portrait Gallery in D.C., and I've honestly never enjoyed going to either of them. I just don't get it. My brain doesn't appreciate it. I like the kind of art where I can look at it and say, "This is a boat on a river. What a nice painting." Or the kind of art you see in humanities class where each person in the painting represents something by the way they are standing or the color of their clothes. I get that kind of symbolism when it is pointed out to me, which is why I enjoyed the art in the Vatican and Sistine Chapel.

However, a friend of mine is a talented artist and many of his works are abstract paintings. I remember a few years back he was showing me one of them in his dorm room. I immediately knew it was well done, I just didn't know what it was supposed to be. I held it in front of me, gave him a smile, and said, "This is really great, man . . . What is it supposed to be?"

He leaned back in his chair and said, "What do you think it is supposed to be?"

I said, "I don't know. Why don't you just tell me what you were thinking when you painted it?"

He laughed, and then he again urged me, "I want to know what you see in it. What does it make you think?"

I said, "Oh. All right."

I gave it another look. I turned it 90 degrees, took a step back, and handed it back to the artist. "I have no clue. Just tell me."

He never did.

A good artist doesn't spell everything out. He leaves it up for interpretation. A great writer leaves a few unanswered questions for the audience. Christopher Nolan to this day won't explain the ending to *Inception*. He's said that viewers who ask about the totem are missing the point of the final scene. It's about the lead character, Cobb, looking at his kids who he'd been trying to get back to for the entire movie.

We want to know the ins and outs of every story and every matter we come across. We don't love hanging endings. But when we understand something completely, it becomes boring and we lose interest.

How many of us sit around and behold the majesty of a number 2 pencil? Who sits for hours and marvels at the wonder of graphite and wood? We understand what makes a pencil. We know what is inside of it and where the materials come from. We know what it does and what it doesn't do. And therefore, no one has paintings of pencils up in their homes.

Yet, we stare into space and try to count the stars and planets. We travel from all over the world to see the Grand Canyon. We hang up paintings of the ocean's billions of scenes. We can't wrap our heads around these wondrous sights and concepts. We don't know every inch of them, so we keep on exploring them. We get lost in their beautiful mysteries. It's more than scenery. It's more than art.

The Bible doesn't exist to point us to indisputable evidence for every question. The Bible exists to point us to Jesus.

It's about Jesus. With all his mysteries and unanswered questions, we'll never understand it all.

Chapter 13

Hamster Prison Break
Why We Have Trouble with Freedom

"Right now we have freedom and responsibility. It's a very groovy time."[1]

Austin Powers

I remember hearing a story from my old youth pastor, Randy, about his pet hamster. His hamster would constantly try to break free and look for chances to run away if they ever took him out of the cage. Hamsters are like little prisoners held against their will, looking for justice and freedom. If you've ever had one, you know they are not usually too fond of their cages.

Note to self—TV show idea: "Hamster Prison Break." A rogue hamster breaks into the cage to free his brother who is addicted to food pellets.

After months of plotting his escape, Randy's hamster finally broke out. They didn't find him for a while, which is every mother's nightmare. Knowing somewhere in your house there is a rodent on the loose who can mate and reproduce at the speed of light. One day they looked behind a bookshelf next to some wires and there was the poor, little hamster. He had chewed through a power cord and electrocuted himself to death.

I know. Gross. But it's a solid lesson.

Three things we can learn here: 1) hamsters are terrible, disgusting pets; 2) no matter how tasty those extension cords look, we mustn't chew on them; and 3) we are more similar to hamsters than we knew we were.

What is it with humans and rules? We hate them. We hate being told what we can and cannot do. The United States was founded on the principle that no one can tell us what to do anymore. My nation is basically one giant middle finger to the East. Some of us are so defiant, we deliberately go against what we are told not to do.

A sausage McGriddle is 429 calories and the absolute worst way to start your day. "I'll take two! #Merica"

We are insubordinate by nature. I'm not sure where this tendency to push the limits came from, but you can trace it all the way back to the beginning of time.

No, not the Garden of Eden. Velociraptors.

Remember the raptors in *Jurassic Park*? Remember what the Australian dude in short shorts who got eaten by them said at the beginning of the movie? The raptors constantly tested the electric fences of their containment area and remembered every piece of fence they had tested. *Jurassic Park* clearly and definitively proves my point scientifically.

The human nature we all live with gives us the tendency to take our freedoms as far as we can and see what we can get away with. Look at toddlers—they are already testing boundaries. What can I get away with? What can I have more of before I get punished?

It's nature. It's science. Clever girl.

People avoid church because when they look from the outside in, all they see are a new set of rules. Don't drink. Don't cuss. Don't sleep around. Give Kirk Cameron movies five-star reviews. People don't like to be boxed in because we are prideful, and we think no one should have any say over what we do.

The truth is, we think way too highly of ourselves. Pride looks at rules and says, "I don't have to follow those." While pride is always at work, I think there is a big misconception about following Jesus. If you look at the teachings of Jesus and only see more rules, you're missing it.

Jesus came to set people free. He came to give you purpose you can hold onto when you lay your head down at night.

Yes, there are some rules, but I think they'd be defined better as boundaries. Boundaries aren't bad. Boundaries protect us. If you've ever leaned over the side of a ship at sea, you're glad there is a boundary holding you back. If you're driving down the road, the boundaries keep traffic from endless head-on collisions.

Boundaries exist all over the place, and they are as simple as actions and reactions. You are free to eat whatever you want and never exercise, but the reaction to your action is out of your control. You are free to jump out of an airplane with a surfboard, but you can't change the rules of how gravity works. You are free to steal the Declaration of Independence, but you can't tell Nicolas Cage not to hunt you down.

Jesus commands us to forgive. You could call that a rule and your pride would naturally want to reject it. Or you could see it as a boundary and realize forgiveness sets you free more than it does the person you are forgiving.

The miscommunication of rules versus boundaries is largely the fault of the church, and it's not an accurate depiction of the good news of the Gospel.

Growing up in the U.S., we constantly hear that America is the greatest nation on earth. It doesn't take long until you believe it like any other law of science. You grow up knowing there is a list of greatest countries in the world, and the United States is always at the top. Usually Britain is second place, because they gave us so much good music, and Hugh Laurie.

For all of the good America does in the world, perhaps America oversteps its rights and overstays its welcome in many cases. We start to think we know what is best for everyone. We start to think the world needs more America. We are the cure.

No matter what we do, our view of the world will always be through an American filter. What are basic civil rights to us may be high privileges to those in other countries. What are bare necessities to us may be luxuries to third world nations. You can rattle off statistics, but you can't truly experience and understand a statistic that you are not a part of.

Does the world need more America in their lives? Does the U.S. really know what is best for the rest of the world?

The church has a similar identity crisis. We overstep our boundaries. We see life through a church filter. Does the church know what's best for everyone? If it does, why do we have so many problems of our own?

What does it mean to spread the Gospel? Does it mean bringing people under a new set of rules? We can look through a church filter and easily think so. We begin to separate ourselves into a new section of rule followers.

It fools us into thinking it's freedom in Christ, when really it is a whole new allegiance to a man-made standard of living.

The book of Acts in the Bible is all about how the first church began. Jesus had been training twelve disciples, and they were in charge of kicking off the church when he left. We only know a limited amount of details about the early church's operation, but it seemed pretty simple. They took care of each other, met often, and devoted themselves to prayer and learning more about God.

It's kind of funny when you look at what the church is 2,000 years later. We have more denominations than you can count. Churches are diverse in how they operate and even in what they believe, yet it all started with one book and one Jesus. But here we are with a global church made up of thousands of churches who don't look much alike other than the fact that we're all singing Chris Tomlin's version of "Amazing Grace" now.

Is this really what Jesus had in mind when he designed the church? You'd think he was a terrible architect. The church was having trouble from day one, hence the majority of the New Testament is made up of letters from Paul and other apostles telling churches how to correct what they're doing wrong.

> *Hey, church in Corinth, get your spiritual gifts under control. Y'all gonna make me lose my mind up in here.*

> *Hey, Galatians, stick to the script.*

> *Hey, Thessalonians, pick somewhere to live that is easier to spell.*

The trouble with the church is that it involves humans. Humans ruin everything. We take the ball and run with it, and then we run off of a cliff. We're all still toddlers by nature. We're velociraptors constantly testing the fences.

We are given freedom, and we abuse it. But does our abuse of freedom make it inherently impure?

A news story broke a little while ago about Disney World. For years, Disney has had a policy which allows people with disabilities to cut to the front of the lines with their families or parties. For many who are physically challenged, it can be difficult to stand in a line for hours on a hot, Florida day. This was just a nice way to lessen their difficulties while still enjoying the parks.

True to human nature, a number of legally disabled people took this freedom and figured out a way to make a profit. They marketed themselves on Craigslist as tour guides who could get families to the front of lines on every ride. Many of the "tour guides" were capable of walking through the park all day themselves. Yet, they figured out they could make $130 an hour, or $1,040 a day. Let's say you did five days a week for a year at that rate, you'd be making around $270,000 a year for going around Disney World.[2]

Is the policy for disabled people wrong because some abuse it?

One of the best albums ever is *The White Album* by The Beatles. In fact it was ranked at number 10 on *Rolling Stone's* "500 Greatest Albums of All Time." The infamous serial killer Charles Manson took The Beatles' masterpiece as a message to himself, though. He mixed random lines from their songs with random verses from the book of Revelation and used it to justify and fuel his terrible acts.

Should the actions of one man who greatly misinterpreted songs ruin the songs for the rest of us?

Just because a freedom is abused or misinterpreted, it does not mean it should be done away with. Airplanes and cars provide us the freedom to travel, and yet they are prone to failure and crashes at the hands of people. Regardless, we still use them daily.

Every form of freedom is abused in the hands of humans. Music. Sex. Alcohol. Even my favorite drug, NyQuil. Someone always figures out a way to take it too far. They test the fences and then break through them.

Have you ever been misquoted, misrepresented, or gossiped about? Has anyone ever taken your words out of context and used them against you? If you have ever had to tell anyone, "That's not what I said," maybe you know a little bit about how God feels.

The church was built on freedom in Christ, and true to human nature, we have seen it abused and misrepresented. The church is in need of constant repair, and it was designed to be this way. It was designed to be a toddler in constant need of the Holy Spirit to help it function in every way. A toddler cannot dress himself, feed himself, or bathe himself. Without the parents, he is just running around naked and hungry. The church is designed to need the Spirit to function for even the simplest of tasks. It is when we start to dress and feed ourselves that we mess everything up.

How many more scandals do we have to hear about in American churches? Every year, a new handful comes to light. Pastors, leaders, and preachers get too full of themselves and start dressing and feeding themselves. It's been happening for ages and will sadly continue to happen.

> Some people enjoy pretending they aren't proud. They worship angels. But don't let people like that judge you. These people tell you every little thing about what they have seen. They are proud of their useless ideas. That's because their minds are not guided by the Holy Spirit. They aren't connected anymore to the head, who is Christ. But the whole body grows from the head. The muscles and tendons hold the body together. And God causes it to grow.

Colossians 2:18-19 (MSG)

Church members in general are constantly guilty of losing connection with the head. We are headless people running around trying to act like everything's normal, feeling around in the dark, chewing on wires, and electrocuting ourselves.

Yet, in all of this madness, we can still see God. We can still experience love, joy, and redemption. It's hard for many to accept that a so-called all-knowing God designed such an imperfect church.

Could it be that God's perfect design is imperfect people?

These days I'm tending to notice a lot of people do not like saying that they are Christians anymore. I think it's because followers of Jesus are kind of embarrassed by what the word *Christian* gets lumped in with nowadays.

I'll admit I'm also embarrassed by a lot of it. Why are Christians known for having some of the most unoriginal music in the world? Why are Christians known for being paranoid about any Democrat in office? Why are Christians known for wearing really dorky T-shirts?

We don't have the best advertisements for our faith. People don't want to be included with the perception of the American Christian. People don't want to call themselves a Christian and have society think they approve of millionaire pastors who drive Bentleys or that they support all Republican candidates just because they are Republicans.

So many Christians keep their guards up against what could be associated with Christianity. And instead of saying, "I'm a

Christian," they proceed to explain the complexities of their faith to you. You are stuck for the next 90 minutes listening to how they think Jesus was a good guy who gets a bad reputation, but the church is out of whack, so they don't want to be included in it.

I read an interview in *Rolling Stone* in which Marcus Mumford of Mumford & Sons was asked about his faith and if he would call himself a Christian. He said this:

> *"I don't really like that word. It comes with so much baggage. So, no, I wouldn't call myself a Christian. I think the word just conjures up all these religious images that I don't really like. I have my personal views about the person of Jesus and who he was. Like, you ask a Muslim and they'll say, 'Jesus was awesome' — they're not Christians, but they still love Jesus. I've kind of separated myself from the culture of Christianity."*[3]

I can understand where Marcus is coming from. Especially in the light of the media and rock scene, which I know nothing about being under. Many artists have to fight off the Christian stigma, or they could get lumped into an entirely different market, missing out on a connection to millions of people they would not otherwise be exposed to. And many Christians are always on the lookout for the next cool Hollywood Messiah to lift up before the masses.

But all of those politics aside, I think Mumford hits on something many Christians who aren't under a media microscope feel about bearing the name of Christ. The problem with saying you follow Christ is that you get connected with the other people who say the same thing, yet don't live anywhere near the way you want to live your life. You get connected with people who abuse the name of Christ and who abuse the freedom he has called us to live in.

We've got a million reasons to want to leave behind the title of *Christian*, which has been misused and stained in so many ways, but I'm not planning on doing it anytime soon.

If you want to call yourself a disciple of Jesus or a follower of Jesus instead of the exact word *Christian* then that's your call. But beyond Christians just leaving behind a word, there is also a desire to separate from the church as well. They don't want the label of Christian, and they don't want to be associated with the people who call themselves Christians.

We have a big problem here.

If you believe in the teachings of Jesus enough to dedicate your life to him, then you also have to love the church. Christ is not disconnected from the church, he is the head of it. Christ is not merely letting those people into Heaven like a bouncer at a bar; he is critically attached to them. And he loves them. He even calls them his bride.

I'm no poster boy for the American church. I think we have a long way to go. And honestly, we'll never totally have it down, because the church is made up of humans, who ruin everything. Just like any other group of people, the church is able to hurt and to be hurt. The church is embarrassing at times, and it is straight up just wrong on some matters. But Jesus loves the church just the same.

You want to follow Jesus, but you don't want to be associated with the church? Well, tough. You are.

I'm not saying we have to stand in defense of every idiot that calls himself a Christian, but if you call yourself a follower of Jesus or any other description you've developed, you are connected to the church. They are your brothers and sisters. There's no way around it.

> *Anyone who claims to be in the light but hates a brother or sister is still in the darkness.*

1 John 1:9

I have a number of friends who are Penn State graduates and I remember watching their football program's awful scandal unfold a while back. The disgust. The pain. The shameful image it brought on the esteemed university. It was nothing short of horrible.

Surprisingly enough, though, I never once saw anyone take down their alumni status online or change the college they graduated from on their résumé. No one made up a new name for the university. They stuck with it. They stood by it. They were associated with it, but they represented the good connected to it. They reminded people that Penn State University is defined by more than just how a few people were currently representing it.

The true function of the church has been distorted, and honestly there were probably about two seconds where it functioned correctly. But should our response be to disconnect ourselves from its bad reputation completely? Or as followers of Christ, should our response be to stand by it? Shouldn't we bear the label of "Christian" and live out what we believe it truly means to be a Christian in the best way we can?

The word Christian is not the only thing that has been distorted. The name of Jesus has been abused as well. Do we leave behind Jesus, too? Or do we do our best to represent him as Christ's ambassadors?[4]

The beautiful thing about true Christianity is we are allowed to be imperfect. Christ wouldn't have died for the church if it were supposed to be flawless. The reason the church has persisted for 2,000 years is because it can take a beating. It can take the ridicule. It can take the hatred. But it keeps going. It doesn't die out. It continues to grow.

I call myself a follower of Jesus. I am called to Christ, therefore I am also called to his people.

I'm a Christian. I'm a rogue hamster who broke out of his cage.

God help me.

Chapter 14

Behind Burned Doors
When My Grandma Dropped the Mic

"What's the matter with you people? You're sad that people are mean? Well, I'm sorry. The world isn't one big liberal arts college campus."[1]

South Park

When I lived outside of Washington, D.C., I attended a megachurch. I never thought I'd be a megachurch type of guy, but they had a service on Monday nights for people in their twenties and thirties, and it was a great fit for me. I got used to not having to wake up on Sundays and go to church, and it was pretty awesome.

That's when I started "Sweatpants Sundays," which is a movement I hope catches on all over the country. What is "Sweatpants Sundays"? Well, it's pretty self-explanatory, but essentially I wear sweatpants and relax after 2 p.m. It's as glorious as it sounds. I rarely go to events or do any work. I may get up and grab dinner, but that's about it. It really helps me rest and reset. Tell your friends. #SweatpantsSundays

At the time I started attending, they had a few different services around D.C., catering to young professionals. These services had their own campus pastor and one teaching pastor who would speak each week just for our services.

During my time there, one of the issues brought to the table by the congregation was that they wanted to have an older generation pouring into their lives. A lot of the members grew up in churches that had older people who helped them grow in their faith. They had people to look up to spiritually. The city has a young population, and especially at a service like ours, many missed having the wisdom of older people in the faith.

After reflecting on this for a long time, the church as a whole made an executive decision to make the young professional's services more like the main church services. They wanted to open it up to people older than twenties and thirties. Also, the main message from Sunday morning by the senior pastor would now be delivered at these services to help bring it all under one roof, so to speak.

I remember sitting there at my Monday night campus when they pitched this idea to everyone in attendance: "This is something we're trying to do to meet the needs we've heard about. This is a bit experimental, too." They were open for discussion and feedback, and I genuinely felt they were trying to do what was best for the church. I honestly didn't mind it at all.

But apparently not everyone felt the same peace I did.

I was sitting in the back of the auditorium when I saw multiple people get up and walk out of the service during the talk from our pastor. Some left immediately, others left at various points throughout. Most were rolling their eyes while walking away.

For some reason, I didn't feel any urge to get up and try to talk any of them out of leaving. My heart didn't break for them. I didn't care to have a discussion about what exactly was upsetting them or why they felt this way. I sat there content to let them walk past me and out of our church community.

If I could go back to that moment, I think I'd let them walk out again. I was annoyed. I thought it was immature to not even hear out a new idea being brought into the community they had been a part of. As a result, I was happy to see them leave, because I thought they were showing their true motives for coming to a church. (I apologize to anyone who got up to use the bathroom who I confused with those leaving the church.)

I know I may sound like the Church Lady right now, sitting on my judgmental throne. But the reason I was happy to see them go is because if someone isn't at least willing to sit through a thirty-minute talk about something like that, then they are coming to church for the wrong reasons. They were expecting the church to be something it is not meant to be.

It's not about you.

It's not about trying to make you happy every week. It gets confusing because many churches cater to the ones who can put in the biggest offerings or who have the most recognizable names.

The Bible addresses this specifically:

> *Suppose a man comes into your meeting wearing a gold ring and fine clothes, and a poor man in filthy old clothes also comes in. If you show special attention to the man wearing fine clothes and say, "Here's a good seat for you," but say to the poor man, "You stand there," or "Sit on the floor by my feet," have you not discriminated among yourselves and become judges with evil thoughts?*

James 2:2-4

The church is something we contribute to; it's not designed to be a place where we only receive. When those people got up and walked out, they were saying, "I'm leaving because I'm only here to receive." Or they could have been saying, "I think I left my car lights on," but I assume it was mostly the former.

The church wasn't designed to serve me and meet all of my intricate specifications. It was designed for me to be a servant.

You should find a community that fits your life and your beliefs well. If your church culture or teachings have changed, you're not evil for leaving to attend a different church. But many people hop around from church to church, or give up in general, because the church isn't meeting their every need and desire. The same reason many people give up on marriages way too easily: "I wasn't happy anymore. It wasn't meeting my needs."

Marriage and church are similar in that neither is designed to meet your needs, and if you go into either of them expecting them to satisfy you, you will be disappointed. If you're only taking, then you're missing the way it works. We all have times where we need to receive something from someone. It's an ongoing process of receiving love, strength, and encouragement, and then giving it back. That's how marriage works. That's how unity works.

Are there some people you can marry who are better for you than other people? Of course. Same with churches. But if you're just a taker, then you won't be a very good church member or a very good spouse.

I heard a story one time from my friend Mike about his four-year-old son who came running in screaming and crying at the top of his lungs. Mike turned and looked at him in horror wondering what could have gone wrong or what had hurt him so badly.

"She wiped spit on me!" yelled the boy about his older sister. Mike went to his daughter and in complete dumbfoundedness asked, "Why would you wipe spit on him?"

His daughter replied, "Dad, it was his spit!"

I know many people who aren't fans of the church these days. They've been burned. They've been silenced, annoyed, and ignored. You name it. And you can lump me into any of those categories as well.

I've been annoyed, burned, overlooked, and ignored. But again, every time I get mad at the church, I have to remember *I am* the church. I have been screaming about spit and meanwhile wiping my own on others.

People can tend to get a chip on their shoulders against the church for some reason or another. They say, "The church burned me," yet they have burned or are burning people all over the place. Some of the biggest complainers I've come across have been the ones who others say have hurt them the most.

Funny how it works. Pride is like staring at the sun. It blinds us from our own faults and the damage we do to ourselves. It makes you the victim.

A far too common reason many churches get started is a result of a church split. One pastor leaves the church and starts another one in the same town with a major chunk of the congregation from the first church. I understand there are reasons why a church may split. Sometimes there may be a need to leave, but I think many of them could be avoided.

Egos are a disease in all of us, and when they get bigger and bigger they hurt us and those around us. Some churches split because a senior pastor has grown too much of an ego and starts acting like a king. Some churches split because someone else's ego has grown and not allowed them to submit to authority.

Pride doesn't handle disagreements. Pride justifies itself. Pride doesn't like being told no.

Who is wiping off your spit while you were complaining about being spat on?

Jesus told a parable in Matthew 13 about the Kingdom of Heaven being like a tiny mustard seed. He said, "Though it is the smallest of all seeds, yet when it grows, it is the largest of garden plants and becomes a tree, so that the birds come and perch in its branches."[2]

A lot of people interpret this parable to mean the Word of God starts out small in us and then grows and makes us strong.

However, this is not how I interpret it. In a few verses before it, Jesus told a parable about seeds being sown on different types of ground. He said the seeds represented "the message of the Kingdom."[3] And he referred to the birds who ate the seeds and said, "The evil one comes and snatches away what was sown in their heart. This is the seed sown along the path."[4] The birds are up to no good in these parables. Alfred Hitchcock was right.

So in the mustard seed parable, I think Jesus was speaking about a ministry, or a church, that can start small and grow into a mighty force. It can provide good to many, but as it grows, the birds will find a place in it, too. You don't have to look far to find birds. Maybe we're more like birds than we realize. And if you've ever seen a statue of any famous person in your town, you know what birds are capable of.

The Christian faith is difficult to live out, because it requires so much humility. It requires us to be constantly lowering ourselves, which is why pride is such an enemy of the church.

Sometimes I feel sympathy for people who are burned by the church. There can be some pretty messed up stuff happening inside of it. I sympathize a lot more with someone who was burned but who never really got involved or wasn't in leadership in any way. Someone who didn't grow up in the church the way I did. I guess I don't hold them accountable, because they were never that involved to begin with. Their reactions could largely be a fault of what people in the church said or did to them, or did not do to include them. And it could all be based off of one or two experiences they had. I feel like they didn't get a decent chance to see the good in the church, so they are not reacting with a truly informed opinion.

But there are some who walk away and speak against their churches who need to just get over their pride.

Many of the burned are at war with something they helped to create. Some of the people I know who are bitter towards the church are people I know who have hurt plenty of others, and yet, they play the victim.

It's like a movie plot where someone's creation they meant for good gets out of hand and they have to shut it down or destroy it. Like in *Jurassic Park* . . . or like in *Jurassic Park 2* . . . or like in *Jurassic Park 3* . . . or like in *Jurassic World*.

There's a story I remember my mom telling me about my grandma, Bernadine Evearitt. (Why is no one named Bernadine nowadays? It's a strong name. I mean, I'm not going to give it to my daughter, but someone else totally should.)

Apparently my grandma was listening to a friend of hers in the church go on and on about how no one else in the church was getting it. He was rambling on about how no one was listening to God the right way and how much he thought was wrong. All the while my grandma listened to him continue to talk.

After listening to more than she could take, she finally said, "Why don't you just put up a cross in the front of your yard and climb up on it, because that's where you really want to be."

Dang, Grandma! She would have dropped the mic and walked away right then, but she never threw anything away.

Some people just want to be martyrs. They play the victim. It's "me against the world," or "me against the church." These people have too much pride to see the truth. Be wary of people who separate themselves.

What has your pride blinded you to seeing? Can you get over it? Can you get over yourself? Are you wiping off your own spit?

Quit being gross.

Some people are burned by the church, and others are burnt out. I'll admit it, the church can be a needy boyfriend who doesn't know when to quit.

> *"We just hung out last night. I need some space."*

> *"You don't mean that. I'm just trying to love you. Why won't you let me love you?"*

> *"I need my alone time and time with my own friends. I need a break, ~~Jon~~ Chris."*

That was just some totally random example I made up.

If you make yourself available to the church, you will usually be used. The problem is most people aren't good at knowing when to cut it off. How else do you think Ben & Jerry's has been so successful? We're not good with limiting ourselves to just a few scoops.

Apparently church burnout has been an issue since the days of the early church. Paul encouraged the Galatians to "not grow weary in doing good."[5]

There's a strange paradox in the church. It's not about you, so you need to serve it. But at the same time, you can serve so much that you start to burn out and lose the reason why you're doing it. I guess it always comes back to balance.

I know people who were super involved with churches and integral parts of the services and community who quit cold turkey after it became too much. What happens is you start getting frustrated with no one else being involved the way you want them to be. You get upset with the leadership. You get upset that you're doing so much. You get tired and weak, and pride loves it when we're tired and weak.

Pride likes to tell you there are many reasons for leaving the church, but the fact is we can find reasons for leaving anything. Pride says, "You're the only one who really cares about this stuff. You're the only one getting it." And then you put a cross up in your front yard and climb up on it.

Do you know why I love Wendy's? Well, there are many wonderful reasons, but one of them is I can go to any Wendy's anywhere and get the exact same meal. The meal I have in Florida will taste the same way it does in Colorado. I don't know how the food industry works, but somehow restaurants are able to replicate their signature tastes all over the country, and even the world. People go back for the consistency. They know what they are getting. Even though you can't get a Double Stack or Jr. Bacon Cheeseburger for 99 cents anymore. Those were the good old days. Thanks, Obama.

The modern church is not like Wendy's where you get the same thing everywhere you go. Some churches don't like fries and only serve baked potatoes. Some churches only serve burgers. Some never refill their ketchup tanks, so you sit there like an idiot wizard trying to conjure up some ketchup from the great below. You're not going to get the same meal at every church. Not even at churches in the same denominations. It's diverse. People are different. You can go to one and hate it and be annoyed by everyone there, but it doesn't mean the church across the street will give you the exact same meal.

The problem is we go to a few churches we don't like and then give up on the idea of church completely. That doesn't make sense, even scientifically. Thomas Edison would be ashamed of this kind of logic and research. "You went to five churches? Talk to me when you've been to 1,000." Reaching a conclusion based off of a few experiences is risky.

I understand the frustration, though. I hate having to compare options. I hate haggling. I hate negotiating. I hate bartering. I hate it all because I'm horrible at it. I'm so bad I can't even wait around on eBay for something. Either I *Buy It Now* or I don't get it. I am miserable in places like Chinatown in New York City where everything is a back-and-forth process of trying to get the lowest price. One of the worst experiences of my life was buying a car.

I hope I'm never responsible for handling a hostage situation.

Me on the megaphone: "Hand over the hostages!"

The bad guys: "We want $20 million and a helicopter."

Me: "Okay that sounds reasonable. Can I get you anything else? A Diet Coke? I'm going to Wendy's anyway."

As someone who is terrible at exploring options, I understand how annoying it can be to go to churches and not feel connected. I understand it makes you want to quit trying altogether. It's tough when you're trying to find the right fit. I only have one pair of jeans, because I have such a hard time finding the right fit. It's exhausting continually being disappointed by churches.

I think you have to accept that a church will never be perfect, because people are not perfect, and you are definitely not perfect.

I know some people who cannot keep friendships, and I know some who have even lost connection with their families. The blame is always on someone else. They talk about how their friends or family left them, stopped contacting them, or hurt them in some way. They're wiping off spit.

Normally if someone loses people in their lives or can't maintain any friendships, it's probably not a sign they have horrible luck in relationships. It shows who the real problem is with, and whose spit it was.

How many more songs can Taylor Swift put out about bad relationships before she gives us a brutally honest hit? Something like, "I Have Commitment Issues and Horrible Judgment."

You can only be the victim for so long, unless you're Lois Lane. If you have a problem with every church you go to, maybe the problem is with you.

Quit being the victim. Victims need hostage negotiators to rescue them. And God forbid I'm sent in to negotiate for you.

When I was a kid, we'd drive up to Virginia to see my Greek grandparents on my dad's side, Papou and Yaya, as we called them. If you've ever seen *My Big Fat Greek Wedding*, my Yaya looked exactly like the Yaya in the movie.

Papou would take my sister and me to the arcade, and then we'd all go to dinner. Papou would always pick up the check. I remember multiple times seeing my parents whisper to each other, and then I'd see one of them distract him while the other one would head back to the table. I was informed years later that they were leaving extra money for the tip, because Papou never left enough.

The Greeks are a proud people, but apparently we're not the extravagant type. I guess we're not the type who would give you fudge on top of your ice cream. The vanilla ice cream is enough as it is. Why would you need any fudge? It's hilarious to me now as an adult to think of how my parents had to go on covert ops to make sure a waitress or waiter received even just 18%.

I realized I've sometimes used my parents' extra tip technique when it comes to my faith in God and my relationship with the church. Sometimes I fear I try to make the church look better than it is. I want to emphasize hope in the church while knowing the shortcomings will inevitably be exposed.

Still, if I believe what the Bible says, and if I believe the Word of God is "living and active,"[6] then why should I try to come back behind the words of Jesus and act like, "Okay, he didn't really mean it like that." Or, "I know what it sounds like, but it's easier than it sounds."

217

Jesus doesn't need me leaving an extra tip on the table. We're dealing with an institution Jesus established. He set up the church and handpicked the apostles who got it rolling. His desire was to have people come together in this manner.

Jesus doesn't need me to make him cool or to make him seem more relatable. Jesus doesn't need me to rephrase what he said, so it doesn't seem as heavy.

We're dealing with Jesus Christ who said stuff like, "Drink my blood and eat my flesh. Take up your cross and follow me."[7] And who spit in the dirt and wiped it on a guy's face.

Jesus turned over tables and ran around with a whip. Jesus said stuff that angered uptight religious people and got laughed at by highly educated people. All to set broken and desperate people free.

Jesus healed the outcasts no one wanted to be around. Jesus spoke to hurting women who were ashamed to be seen in public. Jesus stood up for the poor. Jesus called out abuse when he saw it. Jesus went face-to-face with oppressors.

If I believe what the Bible says, then maybe things need to get a little weird sometimes. Maybe annoying sometimes. There is just no way around it. If we want to know him, then we need to get over it. And we need to embrace his body—the church.

If you want to know Jesus, you can't get around the church. There are no extra tips.

The church. Seriously, what a crazy idea.

The issue here is that we are dealing with a Jesus-instituted idea. He founded the church. He is the architect. He is the contractor. He is the guy on the job site with the clipboard and aviator

218

BEHIND BURNED DOORS

sunglasses. (I don't know much about construction; sorry for the weak analogy.)

Jesus picked a loud-mouthed guy to found it upon. Peter—a guy who didn't make it into college and had to pick up his father's trade as a fisherman. A guy who was terrible at thinking on his feet and was known to use a swear word or two.

Peter didn't really set the bar too high for pastors, or Christians in general, when you think about it. At least not at first. And this is why I love Peter so much. I probably relate to Peter more than anyone else in the Bible.

Jesus believed in messed up, crazy Peter so much that he was the one who changed his name from Simon to Peter the first time they met. Peter means "Rock." And Jesus later told him, "You are Peter, and on this rock I will build my church, and the gates of hell shall not prevail against it."[8]

When Jesus left the apostles in charge, it probably felt like when your parents left you home alone for the first time by yourself. You felt so much freedom and responsibility, and if you were like me, you were also a little afraid. Maybe we need a little more trepidation when handling the church even today.

Maybe we shouldn't be so confident in our own decisions and our abilities to pull off a successful organization of believers. Jesus designed the church to be unable to function on its own, constantly in need of direction from God. Problems arise when we try to do much on our own and too many human efforts and egos get involved.

When the apostles were kicking off the church, they were Jews who had been ministering with Jesus primarily to fellow Jews in their area. They assumed they were just supposed to continue spreading the message of Jesus only to their people. Their church bodies were made up entirely of Jews, and no one really thought anything was out of place. God had to give Peter a specific vision three times in a dream one day.

> *Peter went up on the roof to pray. He became hungry and wanted something to eat, and while the meal was being prepared, he fell into a trance. He saw heaven opened and something like a large sheet being let down to earth by its four corners. It contained all kinds of four-footed animals, as well as reptiles and birds. Then a voice told him, "Get up, Peter. Kill and eat."*
>
> *"Surely not, Lord!" Peter replied. "I have never eaten anything impure or unclean."*
>
> *The voice spoke to him a second time, "Do not call anything impure that God has made clean."*
>
> *This happened three times, and immediately the sheet was taken back to heaven.*
>
> *Acts 10:9-16*

Once Peter woke up, some men were at the door to lead him to Cornelius, who was the first Gentile, or non-Jew, to start following Jesus. From that point on, the Gospel was preached to anyone and everyone who was willing to hear it.

I think it is easy for us to look for the bad. With the rise of the Information Age, we're probably more skeptical now than we have ever been, and maybe rightfully so. There are so many hoaxes out there that fact checking on Snopes has become a normal part of my week. We immediately look for reasons to disagree instead of points where we can agree and come together. It's become our natural reaction.

When it comes to the church, it's easy to see what's wrong with it, especially if you've stepped outside of it. It's not natural to sit down and think about the good when there is so much you can pick apart in the Age of Skepticism. And honestly, much of what gets picked apart is probably accurate. I'm not saying the church doesn't have issues. It has serious issues.

Still, I think the charge God gave to Peter applies even now to the church. Don't call something impure that God has made clean. The church is God's, and through the grace of Jesus, it is holy.

Maybe you don't like the system of the church. Maybe you don't like the music. Maybe you don't like the walls the church can't seem to get rid of. But what are you doing differently while you are spending so much time looking for the bad?

If you start your own rogue church, give it enough time, and it will end up with the same issues many other churches have. Because people will be involved. It's the same way we say we'll never be our parents, and while we do things a little differently, we look in the mirror one day and ask ourselves, "Did I really just use that same line my mother used on me?"

Don't call something impure that God has made clean. Don't call something unholy when God has made it holy. What planks[9] have you missed in your eyes while you were finding the ones in others' eyes? What spit have you wiped on other people?

Can you survive in a relationship with God without attending a church on Sunday? I think so. You could move to a shack on the far side of a mountain and lose all communication with everyone in the world and God would be with you. You would still get a ticket to eternal life whether or not you speak with another person the rest of your life. But what a lonely way to be completely ineffective in your world.

You don't need the church to love Jesus, but you need the church to truly know Jesus.

Martin Luther King, Jr., is credited as the most influential leader of the Civil Rights Movement. He literally led the change of a nation, and he did it all through peaceful protests inside the borders of the country. He didn't lead an army to kill off all the racists; he got legislation changed instead. He proved a revolution could come without war. We still have a long way to go with racism in this country, but his methods and message still resound throughout the nation.

Real, honest change takes time. It can move as slow a glacier. If you want to see the church changed then get some skin in the game. Put some effort in, don't just point out what you don't like.

Don't call anything impure that God has made clean.

We have a long way to go, and it's a goal we will never quite reach. Much like our own development, we'll never be perfect in this life. We'll always miss the mark. The church will always have much to learn and have many ways to grow.

We don't have to be scared of our developmental issues, though, because we have the grace of God.

> But where sin increased, grace increased all the more, so that, just as sin reigned in death, so also grace might reign through righteousness to bring eternal life through Jesus Christ our Lord.

> *Romans 5:20-21*

The scale of sin and grace will always tip in favor of grace. Actually, it will completely collapse on the side of grace.

If we've ever drastically underestimated anything from the Bible, if we've ever miscalculated or misunderstood anything at all, it is the extent and power of the grace of God.

Where any sin abounds, there is more grace.

Any amount of issues, there is more grace.

Any amount of hurt or pain, there is more grace.

Any amount of corruption, selfishness, and pride, there is more grace.

Grace from God falls down with a mighty force like a hammer to a nail. It drives out fear and sin. It changes hearts not through rules, but through love.

Grace washes over our pathetic attempts like a wild, untamable river. There will always be more mercy than mistakes.

By grace we continue to pour ourselves into what Jesus calls us to, even when we begin to feel burnt out.

I believe in the end, the extravagant grace of God is really going to surprise and amaze us. Maybe even anger some uptight, religious people.

Don't call anything impure that God has poured out his grace upon.

This was Grandma as I'll always remember her. Famous for her storytelling.

223

Chapter 15

Please Like Me
When What You Didn't Know Existed
Becomes What You Can't Live Without

"Do I need to be liked? Absolutely not. I like to be liked. I enjoy being liked. I have to be liked. But it's not like this, compulsive *need* to be liked. Like my need to be praised."[1]

The Office

On a chilly evening in Arlington, my life was changed in a single moment.

I didn't go into that moment specifically looking for anything or anyone, and yet, I was found. And even in that first glance, a moment's existence as brief as a raindrop, time was suspended and all of my heart's desires were laid before me. I felt scared and safe at the same time. I felt desire. I felt accepted. In that moment, what I didn't know existed, became what I could not live without.

I'll never forget the first time I saw the Camarones Diablo, the amazing shrimp fajitas at Guapo's Mexican Restaurant.

Did you think I was talking about a girl? I was talking about shrimp fajitas. I'm sorry but they changed my life, and I'll never be the same. It was a moment where I found something my life would not be complete without. My friend Robert and I would go to Guapo's quite frequently with his wife Erica and my sister Melissa. It was love at first bite. And to this day, 90% of the reason I go back to D.C. is for Guapo's. I lie to my friends and tell them I'm excited to see them, but mostly it's for those shrimp fajitas.

It's funny how codependent we become on things we didn't know about just a few moments before. All of a sudden, you can't live without it.

I feel it every time I move and have to start over. When I go to a new church or a new job and see friendships between people I don't know with other people I don't know, I want to have those friendships, too. I immediately want to be accepted.

We've seen an epidemic of codependence with the rise of social media. Never before have we been placed in a popularity contest like this. Twitter shows how many followers you have. Facebook shows how many likes you get. Instagram shows how many meals someone has eaten. It's crazy. I don't even want to talk about the MySpace Top 8 feature. Too many friendships were lost because of it. It's too dark to discuss.

This stuff didn't exist just a few years ago, but all of a sudden, it's become a main source of fuel for our confidence. It sucks when no one likes your photo or reads your posts. Social media is funny because it's like everyone is saying, "Hey, here is everything I'm insecure about!" and then people like it.

Scientific studies have shown that getting a "like" or good comment on something we post increases our oxytocin levels. Oxytocin is what is released when we kiss or hug. I know this because I wrote a report on it in seventh grade. The "like" option didn't exist a few years ago in any form, and now it feeds into our confidence and self-esteem. It's true for most people, but I've seen the following situation play out quite frequently:

> A girl posts a picture of herself, which probably took about 80 attempts to get just right. The girl then finds the right filter and the right angle and posts it on Instagram to be judged and loved by the world. If she's a Christian, she'll include some random Bible verse to somehow justify this selfie. If she's not a Christian, she'll quote Buddha or The Beatles.
>
> The likes start flooding in. The girls start leaving comments like, "Girl, you are so pretty!" "I can't even! Stop!" [Insert random emojis.]
>
> Then the best part is the owner of the selfie comments back like, "Awww, thanks you guys! You're sweet!" It's like they're saying, "Who me? I don't even know how this got posted!"

This is just one example, but we all do it. We all want to be wanted. We want to be noticed. We want to be accepted.

We all have our shrimp fajitas we can't live without.

This need of acceptance goes down to our very cores. We're designed to not be enough on our own. Whenever I hear about people who pulled themselves up by their own bootstraps, I usually don't believe it. Or if they actually did, I believe they are or were lonely people at the time of said bootstrap-pulling. And how does one pull on one's own bootstraps to stand up? How does that even work? I can pull on my shoe strings all I want, but I just lay on the floor and roll around. And who has boots with straps on them anymore? The only person I would believe would have bootstraps is Johnny Depp, because he is just weird enough to have them. And likely they are the ones he saved from *Edward Scissorhands*. That pair the director let him keep. The ones Winona Ryder tried to steal from him when they broke up just because she knew he loved them. And he was all like, "Hey, these are mine. You can have my Pearl Jam tape, because we bought that together, but the boots are mine."

What was I talking about?

Oh, right, we all want acceptance. But we need something stronger than the opinions of Facebook friends and the affirmation of strangers. Those eventually dry up. In Billy Crystal's book *Still Foolin' 'Em*, he talks about how it feels to be a 65-year-old celebrity whose career is not as popular as it used to be. People still know him and love him, but he's not exactly getting pitched the big roles anymore.

> *"Work has brought me great satisfaction and joy. Those situations are fewer now, and there are more and more people telling me I'm not as important as I once was . . . I can't stop conjuring the saddest images my mind can muster, and I'm lost—and then I hear the footsteps running toward me and I hear the giggles, and they yell "Grandpa!" and suddenly they're in my arms and I squeeze them and hold on to them for dear life, and that's a very accurate statement. It is a dear life . . . I am important; I am their star; I am their grandpa."*[2]

We all need love. Billy Crystal has been praised by millions, and if he walks out in public, he's recognized. The Yankees even made him an honorary member of their team. Yet for all of the accolades and awards, it's still not enough to make him feel purpose.

We need love. Deep love. Love that pushes us. Love that scares us. Love that doesn't let us stay the same. Love we must return in the same way.

We need purpose.

A few years back, another one of my favorite Billy's, Billy Joel, was a guest on James Lipton's long-running show *Inside the Actor's Studio*. They discussed his music, his upbringing, and the stories behind his works of art.

At one point in the interview, Billy was asked if he thought he was a good singer. Surprisingly, he replied, "I don't think of myself as a singer. I just don't. I know, and people have said, 'Oh, I like your voice.' I don't like my own voice. I'm always trying to sound like somebody else . . . I'm trying to sound like Little Richard, I'm trying to sound like Ray Charles, I'm trying to sound like The Beatles, I'm trying to sound like anybody but that little schnook from Levittown. I don't like his voice."[3]

With that quote in mind, when you listen to his music now, you may start to pick up on it more. Not just his voice either, but the style of music. *New York State of Mind* was written to emulate Ray Charles. *You May Be Right* sounds like a Rolling Stones song, and he sounds like Mick Jagger. *Uptown Girl* sounds like Frankie Valli and the Four Seasons. It was all intentional.

What's interesting to me is how people now get compared to Billy Joel's voice and music. While imitating others, he became someone who is imitated. But that is how art is supposed to work. It isn't the same thing over and over, but it's also not entirely original.

Art breeds art. True art is always a representation of a previous work in some way or another. I think faith works in the same way. Faith breeds more faith, though it won't look completely identical. Nor should it.

The danger with faith and freedom comes when rules try to lock everyone into a set place. Cathedrals of guilt. Good boundaries turn into binding rules. It happens outside of faith as well, and we end up with two divided sides.

We all know how Congress can be so dysfunctional. I think the main reason is because no one is willing to compromise on anything. Members want their own party's agenda as the only viable solution. My way or the highway. Any functioning relationship doesn't work this way. It's a dictatorship if one person gets their way every time.

America itself is becoming more marginalized every day. We are imitating Congress, which is the worst possible idea. In our need to be accepted and in our search for affirmation, we move farther and farther into one of two extremes. People point fingers at the other side and act like they are classy and above it all, when they are guilty of the exact sins they are accusing the other of. It's like Jesus had a point or something with his "take the plank out of your eye before you go after someone's speck"[4] lesson.

Each side has its own rules to lock you in. You can only have certain opinions and beliefs. The farther you go into any extreme, the louder you hear their message.

Whoever thought it was a good idea to have an outdoor music festival in Central Florida during the summer was insane. Actually doing anything in Central Florida in the summer is kind of nuts. Remember this when you're booking your Disney World vacation. Unless you're boycotting Disney, of course.

One time I went to Warped Tour in Orlando right in the middle of July, and my friend Luke almost had a heatstroke. We spent the majority of the day in the one building with air conditioning with him lying on the ground just trying to breathe and stop the room from spinning. As I was running and getting him another Gatorade, I said, "Luke, aren't you glad you paid $45 for a ticket and also drove us here?" He didn't find it as funny as I did.

When he had finally recovered, we managed to walk around to see a few bands. The stages had been set up all over the fairgrounds and if you stood far enough away, you could hear two different bands at once. It sounded awful. Two emo bands trying to out-complain each other.

To be able to hear the band we wanted to listen to, we had to move into the crowd in front of the stage they were on. We had to smoosh in next to the angsty, sweaty kids in their Hot Topic clothes their parents bought them, but we could actually hear the band clearly.

It's like this when we go deeper into the sides society has divided people into. When we pick which side of the dividing line we are going to stand on. Republican. Democrat. Christian. Atheist. Team Jacob. Team Edward.

You start to hear others agreeing with you, because you're all standing in front of the same band. The message of "Us vs. Them" grows louder and louder. Then the message becomes clearer and clearer as you feel a strength in numbers.

It's easy to confuse this for love, but it's really just agreement. It's not acceptance; it's a shared opinion. And it doesn't last.

What we need can't be found in comment sections and political rallies.

When recognition, in the form of "likes" or short-lived praise, is our fuel for self-esteem, we are in danger. It fools us into thinking it's love, when really it's because we are just standing on the same side of the dividing line as someone else. It's not love. It doesn't change you for the good, and it doesn't satisfy you for long.

When it comes to the extreme sides of issues, people huddle together on either side because it gives them purpose. It feels good to be a part of something. Affirmation of peers imitates love, but just wait until you do something your side disagrees with and see how much love you get. The acceptance you thought you held proves to be shallow. The purpose you want so badly continues to go unfulfilled.

We need purpose. We need to know we matter in this life beyond just holding someone's attention for a passing moment.

I love going to the movies. It feels timeless even though movies have only existed for a hundred years or so. Could you imagine going to the movies back when it was a silent film? I get annoyed just having to read three lines of dialogue in subtitles.

I watched that movie *The Artist* because it won the Academy Award for Film of the Year, and everyone was talking about how good it was. I had to read subtitles the entire movie! For all the cinematic breakthroughs and technological advances we've had in the last century, did someone actually think it'd be a great idea to act like none of that existed? Look Hollywood, if I wanted to read, I'd read a book, and no one likes reading books. You'd have to be an idiot to read a book.

It's interesting how movies have not been a passing fad. Unlike Beanie Babies and fanny packs, they've endured a century and will likely endure the rest of time. We love to be entertained by stories.

But what if you could have your own private movie theater? Everyone wants one of those. Whenever you watch *Cribs* on MTV, and some pop star with only one hit single shows you their house and their private movie theater, you think, *So this is what the American dream looks like. How come I don't have three swimming pools with dolphin butlers? I've done nothing with my life!* It's really cool, but even if I had my own private theater, I think I'd still go see movies in public theaters.

It's not because I love paying half of my salary for a ticket and popcorn. It's not because I love the B.O. smell from the guy sitting next to me who refused to sit one seat away. It's not even because I love fearing my shoes will be ripped off my feet and left behind with every step I take on the inexplicably sticky floor. I think I just like the subconscious feeling of unity I have with complete strangers for 90 minutes.

Movies have a strange power over us even if we don't realize it while watching them. For the length of the film, you and 100 strangers are all watching the same characters. You're rising and falling together with the story. You are in agreement, however strong or weak, for a brief moment in time. It's more noticeable during comedies or funny parts when everyone in the theater laughs together. You're unified without realizing it, even if it just for a few moments. You belong to a crowd for a few hours even though you never speak to anyone.

We chase this subtle kind of affirmation every day, usually without even realizing we are doing it. We are lonely people by nature. I know I am. I talk to inanimate objects if I'm by myself for too long. We're glued to our phones and social media, because it connects us to others at all times and gives us the shallowest form of company. We're disconnectedly connected.

It's an artificial version of purpose and meaning. It's ever-passing, rather disappointing, and the special effects are terrible. It's a distraction from a deeper desire inside all of us.

We chase down distractions in many different forms. Sometimes it's the only way we know how to get through the loneliness of life.

I was always one of the shortest kids in my class. I ate more vegetables than the rest of my peers combined, but it didn't matter. I always got, and still get, the short jokes. It's not so bad nowadays because people will get fired and berated by the PC social media activists if they ever say anything about anyone's physical features. But growing (or not growing) up I was reminded daily. Many times it wasn't comments from people deliberately trying to hurt me. They were just making stupid remarks about my height, but it still hurt.

I think it's one of the reasons I tried being funny and started writing joke songs. I wanted to be known as the funny guy instead of the short, quiet, awkward guy. Many of the tall and good-looking types know nothing about the struggle for acceptance. We short, awkward people, who uncontrollably sweat too much, have to earn it. This is why a lot of people who have been good-looking their entire lives and are just effortlessly popular have the personalities of rice cakes.

I still struggle with insecurity about my height. A long time ago I was feeling discouraged, so my mom talked to me about the insecurities she had growing up. She was cross-eyed until she was 20 years old and finally had corrective surgery, so she grew up enduring a lot of ridicule from her peers. She said she cried a lot. She spent a lot of time hating the way she looked and trying the best she could to deal with the hurtful things people would say about her. It's tough enough being a kid without having to deal with physical features that draw unwanted attention to you.

My heart still breaks when I think about a little, innocent girl who was defenseless against the attacks. Just a kid who wanted to be accepted for who she was, not how she looked.

Maybe we're all cross-eyed kids on the playground in some way or another. Lonely. Scared. Holding back the tears as best we can, and maybe failing to do so. Looking for a friend. Looking for a voice to speak up for us and defend us. Looking for acceptance and purpose beyond the world's opinions.

My mom told me, "You know, I remember when I was all alone in my room at the end of the day, feeling like no one loved me and no one wanted me, I would think, 'Well, at least I know Jesus loves me. Jesus made me and loves me just like he made me. Jesus knows me, likes me, and wants to be my friend.'"

In her loneliest moments, she had hope. She found true purpose. True security.

Jesus came for us lonely children trying to fit in. The ones who run home in tears. The proud aren't looking for him, because they don't think they need him. But for those of us who need a voice and a defender, who need to know we matter—he's our friend.

He's our purpose when the world hasn't accepted us. He's our purpose when no one else wants what we have to offer. He says we're wanted when our best isn't good enough for anyone else.

Jesus loves you.

That statement sounds so overused and played out sometimes, but it shouldn't be robbed of its truth and power.

Jesus loves you. Just as you are. You have purpose. You matter. You belong. You have a place. You have hope. You are wanted. And you never have to be alone again.

The Bible is not a rulebook. That's hard for many people to understand. It's hard for me to accept, too.

Having grown up in church, I developed a subconscious view of how both blessing and cursing work. I wrestle against the idea of a "cause-and-effect Gospel."

When my life is good, I think, *Well, it's because I am reading my Bible every day and giving money to the poor.* When my life is not so good, I start to think, *Alright, God. How did I upset you? Was it because I watched* The Matrix, *and it's rated R? But Neo is supposed to represent Jesus!*

I've sat through countless hours of church and youth group retreats and heard about how I need to be doing more to deny myself and chase God. And it's true. Jesus gave some big challenges about taking up our crosses and following him. As a result, I struggle with being at peace with God. If I ever feel happy, my knee-jerk reaction is to think, *I shouldn't become complacent. I need to be pushing myself. What sin am I not addressing?*

This is the wrong approach to God, because it puts a focus on what I need to be doing. I want to be affirmed by God, and it pushes me farther into one side—the side I think God will be most happy with me being on. Really I'm looking for a form of affirmation from God which doesn't exist. I'm looking for the list of rules I've followed to be checked off, given a gold star, liked, and retweeted. Rules I've written for myself.

I sometimes wonder if I would have made it into any of the Gospels if I'd been around while Jesus was walking the earth. I wonder if I would have been too scared to be his disciple. I wonder if I would have understood he was the Messiah, or if I would have laughed in his face. From studying the Bible, I know what Jesus did and who he was, but I wonder who I would have thought he was if I was watching the Gospel story unfolding before my eyes.

I honestly think Jesus may have annoyed me in some ways. Yeah, I said it.

The main reason I think Jesus may have annoyed me is because you couldn't seem to get many straight answers when you asked him a question. He would answer your question with another question. Jesus asked 307 questions that were recorded in the Bible. That's a lot of questions to have in just a few short pages. Seems to me he was big on getting our minds and our hearts working together and not so big on spoon-feeding the answers.

Jesus was the artist who wouldn't tell me what the painting was. He would make me figure it out for myself.

His message was spread through different men and women, each with a different personality. No one had a rule book. Jesus came in and freed everyone from the burden of the Law, and back then they didn't have a new 12-step "Life with Jesus" pamphlet to follow. They had to figure it out as they went. And they got some stuff wrong. They disagreed on issues. They sounded stupid. They changed their minds.

The Gospel is an art that is meant to spread and stretch in the hands of ordinary people. There may be some boundaries, but there is much freedom. And there is even more grace.

Our acceptance should not be determined by how much we line up with a certain group, or how deep we can dive into a church culture. Our acceptance, affirmation, and purpose are built on grace. We are the ones Jesus wants.

> *Therefore be imitators of God, as beloved children. And walk in love, as Christ loved us and gave himself up for us, a fragrant offering and sacrifice to God.*
>
> *Ephesians 5:1-2*

What does it mean to imitate Christ?

Don't tell us. Show us. Go figure it out. Dive into grace. Take chances. Make mistakes. Get messy!

Wait, that's the quote from *Magic School Bus*. I can't end this chapter with that. Let me try again:

Jump in the mud. Get your hands dirty with love.

Okay, that's Dave Matthews Band. Whatever, I'm leaving it in. By the way, if Dave Matthews ever invites you onto his magic school bus, you probably should just walk away.

Chapter 16

Stick of Dynamite
What Side is Jesus On?

"I guess all's well that ends well."
"Doesn't matter to me, as long as it ends."[1]

The Great Muppet Caper

I wish I still got yearbooks. The kind of yearbooks you get in high school, full of pictures and memories. Pages and pages of names you'll never forget, and ones you never could remember to begin with. I'd like to have one for each year of my life. We definitely take enough pictures now to document every second of our lives, but the best part of yearbooks to me wasn't the pictures. It was the signatures.

It was always fun to have people sign my yearbook and see who wanted me to sign theirs. I was looking at some of my old yearbooks all the way back to elementary school, and back then we all just signed our names, because we'd just learned how to spell them. I noticed as the years progressed, my friends' signatures started to get a little more elaborate, and they started including more meaningful memories and comments. Of course I would still get the traditional "stay sweet" from girls and "have a great summer" from guys who couldn't think of anything better to say.

Just so you know, I did have a good summer, and I've also decided I would like to stay sweet. So thanks for the advice. Powerful stuff.

Sometimes I wonder what God would say to me at the end of every year. I wonder what he'd write in my yearbook. Would it be like when you got a teacher to sign it who wasn't quite sure who you were?

"You were one of my students. Keep learning. Math is power."

I wonder what he'd write in mine as my life and spirituality progresses. Would it grow more meaningful year after year the way my old yearbook signatures did?

Maybe some years he would say, "Keep doing what you're doing." Other years he might write, "You have a long way to go." Or, "You worry too much. KIT. HAGS." I think every year he'd write something different, because each year is different. If you ever relive the same year, you are either in some kind of *Groundhog Day* scenario, or you are not growing.

Life is not meant to be relived, it is meant to be lived. Faith is not only a study of what has been, it is an exploration into the unknown.

What is God signing in your yearbooks?

My faith has progressed and will continue to progress. I learn more and more about God and the world every day. My views about culture and politics change. My concepts change. It's a never-ending process of improvement and refinement. I am continually chasing down who I want to become while simultaneously still figuring out who exactly it is I want to become.

Speaking of writing in books, I write a lot in my Bible. Some people don't, but I think everyone should. I underline verses. I write little notes of what I think God is revealing to me and teaching me. I put down my interpretation of a passage. I leave encrypted messages in case Nic Cage ever steals it.

I also have a lot of thoughts I've scratched out from over the years in the margins. At first it annoyed me, and I felt like I was cluttering up the pages, but I've come to enjoy seeing the scribbles and erase marks. It shows me I am still growing in God, my views can change, and God is still God.

I don't think God changes, but my approach to God changes quite often. I'll never say, "I get it. I have figured God out." And with my changing approach to God, it means I will often change my approach to his church and the rest of the world.

I'm not a perfectionist. I want to pursue perfection, but I just make too many mistakes to ever come close to calling myself a perfectionist. Some people tell me they are perfectionists, and then I look at what they produce and think, *Wow, you have really low standards of perfection.*

The truth is, there is no such thing as a perfectionist in faith and church. There are people pursuing perfection who think they may have obtained it, but in time, they realize they have not. Then they find a new form of perfection to pursue. They are really just chasing down what they think perfection looks like.

I'm not chasing perfection in my church experience. If I were, I'd never be able to live with myself. I'm too incomplete. I'm too much of a mess, and the church is too much of a wreck for a perfectionist to ever have anything to smile about. We'll never get anything right until we can accept that we've probably got some things wrong.

I keep coming back to the same question I mentioned earlier. Do I trust God enough to be wrong?

It can be scary to think we have some wrong ideas about God and church and life and love, especially if you think you're a perfectionist.

Do you trust God enough to be wrong? Are you humble enough to admit when you are?

I didn't realize adult life would contain so many acronyms. How many acronyms am I supposed to remember? It's insane. People spit them out to me like I'm supposed to know what they mean. My usual response is to nod my head like I know what they're talking about and then go look it up later. I wish I was joking.

Who can remember them all?

HMO: Health Maintenance Organization
AWOL: Absent Without Lettingusknow
BYOB: Bring Your Own Bae
OPEC: Oil People Eating Cookies

Well, I have one more for you to remember. TBU: True But Useless.

I recently had the opportunity to listen to Dan Heath[2] speak at a conference I was attending. Dan spoke about change and used a story from his book *Switch* about a man named Jerry Sternin who worked for Save the Children in 1990. The Vietnamese government had brought him over to help fix the malnutrition problem affecting millions of their children. And they wanted him to do it in six months.

They had concluded the malnutrition was a result of poor sanitation, nearly universal poverty, a lack of access to clean water, and a common ignorance about nutrition among the rural communities. Jerry Sternin recognized these facts as TBU. He'd never be able to fix the poverty situation on his own or improve the other major issues, especially in six months.

He had to find what Dan Heath called "bright spots."

Sternin found out a few mothers in a local village had healthy children, so he looked into what they were doing differently with their children. Surprisingly enough, the difference was not because they had more money, more education, or more prominent friendships. They were simply doing things a little differently.

The malnourished children ate twice a day. The mothers of the healthy children were feeding their kids four times a day, using the same amount of food as other moms, but just spreading it out over four meals. The malnourished stomachs couldn't efficiently process the larger servings of food as well as they could if the meals were smaller. The mothers also fed their children crabs, shrimp, and sweet potato greens, which were commonly thought to only be adult foods.

Heath said that Jerry Sternin found the bright spots and then repeated them. He found the good and then replicated it. He didn't have to change the major sanitary issues; he found a way to get around them. By the end of his six-month assignment, 65% of the kids were better nourished. They began to implement the new diet all over the country and millions of children lived better lives because of the bright spots.

This story immediately made me think of the church. Critics of the church have gathered a lot of TBU facts. We know what the church is wrong about in so many ways. We know how out of touch Christians are. We know how cheesy so many ministry endeavors are. And it's important to recognize them.

In the end, though, that kind of data is mostly TBU. We sit around with our score cards and do nothing. We must find the bright spots and then do something about them.

Some people want to fix the church all at once. It's the same idea people get about politicians who they think will come in, flip a switch, and America will work perfectly. Neither of these is possible, because mass change doesn't work this way. What if, instead, we looked for the good and then followed Jesus' advice to "Go and do likewise"?[3]

For all the church is getting wrong, there has to be some stuff it is getting right. If you cannot find any bright spots in the church, then you are not looking hard enough, and your data is incomplete.

Still, when we look at the massive amount of change it needs, it can feel like trying to move a mountain by moving one handful of dirt at a time. It makes you never want to even try. It's overwhelming to try and change everything at once, but little by little, one by one, change happens. Bright spots can be replicated.

Get rid of the TBU and get involved. No one yelling from the bleachers changes the score of the game. Whether you are inside of the church or outside of it, you are meant for more than opinions and useless chatter.

I don't consider myself a runner, mostly because I hate every second of running. Some people run to see how far they can run. I run so I can eat ice cream and burritos. I wish I had more of a motivation, but sadly that is pretty much it.

I especially cannot stand running on treadmills. Treadmills are one of those things that somehow slipped through the cracks of ridiculousness, and now everyone thinks they are normal. If some dude from the 1500s traveled to our time and saw us running in place while watching CNN on a muted TV in the corner of the room, he'd say, "You people are idiots. This is even coming from a guy who just lit a woman on fire, because we thought she was a witch . . . And CNN? Really?" We run on treadmills but go nowhere. I can almost tolerate running outside. I like the changing scenery. I like not having to stare at how far I've gone on a blinking screen in front of me every second of the run and watch my heart rate soar higher and higher.

One hot Florida day I was on a run with my wife, but we also had to pick up some birthday candles, because it was a friend's birthday, and Brittany had made a cake. So we decided we'd run to Walgreens and back, and then I could carry the bag while I ran like I was Barry Sanders or something. (By the way, this is sad proof of how little I pay attention to sports nowadays. Barry Sanders, who has been retired since 1999, was the first running back who came to my mind.)

The heat of the day took more out of me than I realized it would, and by the time we got to Walgreens, I needed some water badly. I immediately went to the water fountain at the back of the store to quench my thirst. As I dipped down, I expected some cool, refreshing water, but instead I got warm, bitter, sadness. It was disgustingly hot water. I spit it out immediately. It was like trying to drink a Jason Derulo song.

The church can tend to have this same effect on people who come running to it and expect something refreshing. They are thirsty, tired, and looking for hope. Instead of being restored, they are hit with warm, terrible water. And what they need is Living Water.

A church can have all the pomp, flair, and presentation of a U2 concert, but if there is no deeper substance than a performance, it's just like people running on treadmills. Putting forth a ton of energy and going nowhere.

The pageantry and special effects are attractive and perhaps useful in some instances, but if people are only attending because of these reasons, then there is nothing deeper connecting them to Christ and the church community. People are running on treadmills and spitting out disgusting water.

> *"Come, all you who are thirsty,*
> *come to the waters;*
> *and you who have no money,*
> *come, buy and eat.*
> *Come, buy wine and milk*
> *without money and without cost.*
>
> *Why spend money on what is not bread,*
> *and your labor on what does not satisfy?*
> *Listen, listen to me, and eat what is good,*
> *and you will delight in the richest of fare."*
>
> *Isaiah 55:1-2*

It's a shame to waste our energy on unsatisfying food and offer the world nothing more than bitter water when Jesus offers so much more.

The church has an incredible amount of potential and power packed into it. It's like a stick of dynamite. Dynamite is used to break down barriers and create new pathways. It has taken us deeper to resources in the earth. But it has also been used for destruction of good. It has destroyed lives.

Some of the energy of the church sits unused and ineffective. Forgotten about. It's useless, really.

Some of the energy is used for good. Widows and orphans are taken care of and fed. The naked are clothed. Broken lives receive hope and joy and friendship. Communities are served. New life is found.

Some of the energy is used inappropriately and supposedly done in the name of Jesus. It blinds the weak and binds others in fear. It stands in defiance in places it never was meant to stand. It cuts deep wounds that never get healed. It turns the hearts of men and women away from the love of God.

The church is a stick of dynamite sitting in the hands of ordinary people.

There are two sides to choose from—the church or the world. There is a line dividing the two options, and we must pick one side to be on.

It sounds so extreme, but it's the only options we seem to be given by the screaming voices on both sides. Each side is angry with the other side for not being open-minded, and both are refusing to hold a mirror up to themselves.

However, I still believe there is a way to walk between the two.

The dividing line is so thin it's almost unnoticeable. Like a tightrope stretched in between, it runs down the line through all the noise and anger. It travels narrowly through the miscommunication, misperception, misrepresentation, and grey areas.

This is the line I want to spend the rest of my life walking on. This line between the church and the world. It terrifies me. It makes me second guess my thoughts and statements. The extremes of both sides are vicious and waiting for people to make mistakes, so they can catch them in it.

Walking the line seems impossible at times. Walking on this tightrope can be so frustrating I want to give up and fall off to one side, and then go deeper and deeper into the noise. Deeper into the crowd. So deep that I don't ever have to hear the other side or have my opinions challenged again. Where I could surround myself with the loudest voices and cling to their message.

But I want to walk down this line, because Jesus walked it. Jesus stood on the tightrope and moved forward on it.

He wasn't afraid of it. He didn't live a double life or try to fool anyone into thinking he wasn't walking it. He lived his life between the two sides. He was reserved and bold. He was sympathetic and unapologetic. He was compassionate and challenging. He was merciful and direct.

He was love. He is love.

Maybe this line is the straight and narrow road he spoke of when he said, "Enter through the narrow gate. For wide is the gate and broad is the road that leads to destruction, and many enter through it. But small is the gate and narrow the road that leads to life, and only a few find it."[4]

Society as a whole has never liked the line. It makes you look indecisive or not dedicated enough. Neutral. When the fact is, it is anything but neutral. Neutral means you have no opinion about anything. The line doesn't mean you're neutral. You're not neutral, because you do not devote yourself entirely to one of the two loudest choices given to you. You don't have to devote yourself to a side.

You can devote yourself to God.

It's a devotion to a world Jesus wants to save, and a church he wants to save just as badly. I want to walk this dividing line, because I find it to be the most straight and narrow of roads. It's possible to walk it. We will make mistakes. We will eat our words. We will be hypocrites. We will give up and then get back on it. And we will find life and purpose. We will live out love.

I wonder what God sees when he looks at this situation. Maybe he doesn't even see a dividing line or any sides at all. Maybe he just sees his children. And he wants everyone to come to him. He wants a personal relationship with every single person, no matter which side we think we are on.

When we find ourselves in the mix of it all, between a modern-day church and a modern-day world, we find ourselves closest to the cross.

The cross of Jesus intersects the church and the world.

The cross unites heaven and earth.

The cross was beautiful and ugly.

The cross was utterly shameful and the most honest act of love ever displayed.

The cross was pain and glory.

The cross is where all the hopelessness of mankind was completely crushed by the grace of God.

God has placed the hope for the world, this stick of dynamite, in the hands of ordinary people. Stupid, selfish, broken people. People who speak before they think. People who get in the way. People who don't know when to quit. But people with enough potential to love beyond reason.

It's going to be messy, confusing, challenging, and even painful. It's also going to be beautiful.

Epilogue

When I was a kid, we had some pretty ugly furniture in my home. My grandma had a pink couch and a matching pink chair that she'd given us when she updated her furniture. You should know it's not a good sign when you not only have the same furniture as your grandparents, but it's something they even wanted to get rid of.

The pink chair had high armrests so you'd sit there with your arms up by your head looking like you still had your hanger stuck in your shirt. This chair would basically swallow up any human who sat in it.

As tacky as it was, it often became more than a man-eating chair to me. I would take the seat cushion and push it up between the armrests, and then I'd throw a blanket over the top. Suddenly I was secure within the walls of my fort. I'd peek through the blanket at my family as they walked by and wonder if they knew anyone was in there. (They did.) I'd do most of my best thinking in my fort.

The creativity we have as children is quite impressive. Somehow, we entertained ourselves by taking ordinary objects and recreating them with our imaginations. Bedrooms become kingdoms. Trees become fortresses. Little brothers become giant baby dolls who you can dress up and paint their nails. (Or so I've heard.)

Children's creativity is one of the clearest examples to me of how we are made in God's image. I think about how God created man, and it was quite similar.

> Then the Lord God formed a man from the dust of the ground and breathed into his nostrils the breath of life, and the man became a living being.
>
> Genesis 2:7

God took something as simple as dust, breathed into it, and here we are today. The ability to see something as more than it is comes straight from God. Maybe Jesus wanted the children to come to him, because he wanted to be with people who see life more like he sees it.

I wonder what God sees when he looks at his children.

We see a failure, and he sees a world leader. We see weakness, and he sees strength. We see a lost cause, and he sees restoration.

God makes new creations out of ordinary things. Think of the potential the church must have under the vision of a creative and loving God like this. He breathed life into dust, so think of what he could create out of willing and open hearts.

I've stated numerous frustrations about the church in this book, but I hope you have heard my heart above the critiques. I really do believe in the church and in its people.

I get frustrated when I feel the church is misrepresented, or even at the ways I have, and will, misrepresent it. I am by no means an expert; I'm not even a pastor. I didn't go to Bible college, and I could walk through the halls of any church in

America and go unrecognized. Still, I believe I have a voice. It may not be a voice that reaches millions, but maybe I don't need to have my own cable show to make a difference. Maybe the difference God wants me to make has nothing to do with pulpits or headlines.

My friend Steffan and I were working on this book when he told me that he's made peace with the misrepresentations of Jesus. He said it's more meaningful to tell people what he actually believes instead of saying, "I'm a Christian," and then having them associate it with whatever Christian stereotype is already in their heads. I like that a lot.

The truth is, what Christianity looks like today is not what it looked like 2,000 years ago. It's not what it looked like 200 years ago, and it likely won't look like this 200 years from now. In fact, even presently, Christianity looks different all over the world. So why should we let someone else identify our beliefs for us?

Why should we shy away from telling people what is on our hearts? So many other people are quite willing to share their views with the masses constantly. I know this because I am on social media, and it's an election season, and if I had a nickel for every Bernie Sanders meme I've seen I could pay for everyone's college tuition and build a wall.

I'm not out to change the world. It's too big. But I'm up for changing *my* world.

I'm up for having some conversations that go late into the night. I'm up for spending a little time outside of my comfort zone and seeing what comes of it. I'm up for listening more than I speak.

All I have to offer is the dust I've been made from. But in the hands of the Creator, I can't wait to see what he creates with it.

So . . . did you enjoy this book? I hope so.

If you did, please write a review on Amazon.com. Believe it or not, something that will take you three minutes could have a massive impact on this book spreading farther. You don't even have to write an essay, just a sentence.

Thank you!

Acknowledgements

God, thanks for letting me write about you and loving me in spite of what I get wrong.

Brittany, thanks for marrying me, believing in me, pushing me, listening to me, and so much more that I can't find words for. You've heard me repeat the same stories and jokes countless times trying to see what connected. I know you've heard more about this book than you ever cared to. You're kind, patient, and quite pretty.

Mom, thanks for being who you are. You've never doubted me even when I doubted myself. Thank you for letting me live a creative life and being at every basketball game, comedy or music night, and any other thing you believed in me to try. And thank you for most likely buying 300 copies of this book.

Melissa, thanks for letting me live with you so I could get that good story about the A/C repairman in here. I owe my D.C. years to the kindness of you and Nick. Thank you for giving me your hard-earned cash when you were 20, so I could buy a new guitar. You've always looked out for me when you weren't trying to beat the crap out of me. I still value your opinions much higher than I even want to. Forever your little brother. And I can't wait to meet my niece!

Dad, thanks for making me grow up in church and giving me a lot of material for this book. And for not suing me over content issues. I hope you're proud.

Scott, thank you for seeing something in me at 19 and making an eternal investment. Thank you for giving me a few different types of microphones and stages and the freedom to see what happened next. Looking forward to the future and what we'll try out.

Pastor Carl Thompson, you are well-remembered, and I pray your legacy and heart has been represented in these pages because so much of who I am is a result of your love and labor. You always had time to meet with me in your office, and I know you always had me in your prayers.

Maria West, you put more work in on this than I can even comprehend. I kept waiting for you to tell me to quit writing for good, but your commitment to this project and this message was nothing short of amazing. You up for book number two? Well, maybe just think about it for now.

Sara Thompson, you were the first to take on this project, which was such a blessing. Thank you for all your edits and encouragement!

Sam Mitchell, Josh Evans, and Britt Daniel, thank you for your stellar edits, suggestions, and for the hours you poured into this thing. Group road trip soon?

Steffan and Laura Clousing, I don't even know where to begin. Your support means the world to me, and I know we're just getting started. Laura, you were the very first person to tell me you thought I was supposed to write a book one day. Funny how it finally happened and how you and my new BFF Steffan were involved. You've been so impactful. Steffan, I can't thank you enough for all the hours you poured into this thing, your design work and late nights figuring all this stuff out.

Carlene Garboden, thank you for all of your edits and doing far and above what we originally discussed. You should have known after 25 years what you were getting into, though. That's not my fault. Looking forward to future projects!

Swain Strickland, thank you for your feedback and website building skills. I know how annoying the process can be. And thank you for your lawnmower which I don't think I ever paid you for. It completely broke, though, so . . .

Brandon Noel, thank you for your feedback and encouragement and for letting me use our stories in this book. Chris Cervellera, thanks for all the meals over the years. Our group text will never end.

Ocean City Church and River City Church, thank you for the encouragement and giving us a place to call home here in Jacksonville. I feel like so much of OCC & RCC ended up in these pages.

Author Launch, thank you for an amazing program that helped me get my book moving and finished. I learned a lot and can't believe this finally happened.

Bono, thank you for proving that you can love Jesus and also not be the weirdest person in the room. Also, if you see this, I'd love some tickets to the next tour.

Kirk Cameron, thanks for being able to take a joke. Or seven of them. Lunch sometime?

Walter the Dog, thanks for smelling my feet every day while I wrote this and never asking me to change the music.

And finally, thank you to anyone who bought this book and was curious enough to read this section. You make me feel better about myself, because I read this type of stuff, too.

Notes

Chapter 1 Inside Outside

1. Rosenthal, Philip, Steve Skrovan, and Ray Romano. "Just a
    Formality." *Everybody Loves Raymond*. CBS. 3 Feb. 2003. Television.
    Transcript.

Chapter 2 Don't Mess with the Formula

1. Lewis, C.S. *Mere Christianity: A Revised and
    Enlarged Edition, with a New Introduction, of the
    Three Books the Case for Christianity, Christian
    Behaviour, and Beyond Personality*. New York:
    Macmillan, 1952. Print.
2. Originally I thought this was called a Mosaic, but during the editing
    process my friend pointed out that I had written this completely
    wrong. Clearly I'm not expert in art, but the point is solid.
3. See Hebrews 10:25.
4. *The Lion King*. Buena Vista Pictures Distribution, Inc., 1994.
    Transcript.
5. John 15:19.

Chapter 3 Silent Monk Screams

1. Rowling, J.K. *Harry Potter and the Goblet of Fire*. New York: Scholastic, 2000. Print.
2. See Colossians 1:18.

Chapter 4 Hollywood Moses

1. Ricketts, Harry. *Rudyard Kipling: A Life*. New York: Da Capo Press, 2001. Print.
2. According to IMDb, Saving Christmas is now at the number 2 spot. It got beat out by *Code Name: K.O.Z.* in 2015. I'm actually surprised, and proud to say, that I haven't seen any of the movies on this 100 list and never will. We have to stand for something, right? http://www.imdb.com/chart/bottom
3. All fan reviews are from Fandango.com.
4. Matthew 11:11.

Chapter 5 My public Meltdowns

1. Conan O'Brien in his 2011 commencement address to Dartmouth College. www.youtube.com/user/teamcoco/
2. See Matthew 5:14.
3. "Blinded By the Light," written and performed by Bruce Springsteen. circa 1973. Most popular version is Manfred Mann's cover of it in 1977.
4. See John 8:10-11.
5. John 8:12.
6. David, Larry, Jerry Seinfeld, Tom Gammill, and Max Pross. "The Glasses." *Seinfeld*. NBC. 30 Sept. 1993. Television. Transcript.
7. Luke 4:18-19.

Chapter 6 Chili's, Bennigan's, and Other Places I Wasn't Allowed To Go

1. *Finding Nemo*. Buena Vista Pictures Distribution, Inc., 2003. Transcript.
2. *Cool Runnings*. Dir. Jon Turteltaub. By Lynn Siefert and Michael Ritchie. Perf. John Candy, Leon, and Doug E. Doug. Walt Disney Pictures, 1993. Transcript.
3. Toalson, Art. "The Disney Boycott: A Slow but Certain Influence." *SBC Life*. Southern Baptist Convention Executive Committee, 2016. Web. 15 May 2016.
4. See Matthew 7:15.
5. Lipton, James, and Robin Williams. "Robin Williams." *Inside the Actors Studio*. Prod. Michael Kostel. Bravo. New York, NY, 10 June 2001. Television.
6. Proverbs 1:7.
7. Romans 11:20.

Chapter 7 Zacchaeus

1. *The Naked Gun: From the Files of Police Squad!* Dir. David Zucker. By Jerry Zucker and Jim Abrahams. Perf. Leslie Nielsen. Paramount, 1988. Film.
2. Luke 19:8.
3. Luke 5:31.
4. 2 Corinthians 5:21.

Chapter 8 Church in a Bar

1. Fey, Tina. "Best Actress TV Series Musical or Comedy." *66th Golden Globes*. NBC. Los Angeles, CA, 11 Jan. 2009. Television.
2. Proverbs 20:5.
3. Matthew 18:20.

Chapter 9 The Exaggerated Battles of American Christians

1. Stewart, Jon, Ben Karlin, and David Javerbaum. *America (the Book): A Citizen's Guide to Democracy Inaction.* New York, NY: Warner, 2004. 107. Print.
2. Begala, Paul. "Begala: The Day Jon Stewart Blew Up My Show." *CNN.com.* N.p., 12 Feb. 2005. Web. 27 May 2016.
3. Revelation 13:1.
4. See 2 Timothy 1:12.
5. See John 18:37-38.
6. 1 Peter 2:17.

Chapter 10 Identity Crisis

1. Medieval legends claim that the Holy Stairs were brought from Jerusalem to Rome about 326 by St. Helena, mother of Constantine the Great. In the Middle Ages, they were known as Scala Pilati or "Stairs of Pilate." And I read that on Wikipedia, so it must be true.
2. See Hebrews 10:38.
3. This was written before Donald Trump was an actual candidate people were voting for. Still, the logic hold soundly because the RNC was doing everything they could to block it and get one of their guys in. If you're reading this in the future, I'm sure President Trump has made America great again, and the wall is 500 feet high, and everything is perfect.
4. See Luke 14:23.

Chapter 11 Full House Lied to Me

1. *Forrest Gump.* Dir. Robert Zemeckis. By Eric Roth. Perf. Tom Hanks, Robin Wright, Gary Sinise, Sally Field, and Mykelti Williamson. Paramount Pictures, 1994. Transcript.
2. See Genesis 12:1-9.
3. See Genesis 28:1-21.
4. See Genesis 37-41.

5. See Exodus 2-3.
6. See 1 Samuel 21 and a ton more chapters and Psalms.
7. See 1 Kings 19:9.
8. See Matthew 3.
9. See Luke 4.
10. See Judges 6:13.
11. See Judges 6:14-15.
12. See Judges 6:13.
13. See Matthew 9:18-26. Peter did this as well in Acts 9:36-42.
14. 1 Corinthians 13:12.
15. See Exodus 33:12-23, Exodus 34:33-35, and 2 Corinthians 3:7-18.

Chapter 12 God Did It

1. Milne, A.A. "In Which Piglet Does a Very Grand Thing." *The House at Pooh Corner*. London: Puffin, 1928. N. pag. Print.
2. Even as I write this I am listening to the Interstellar soundtrack. That movie really makes me miss my children even though I don't have any.
3. White, Candace, and Robert Booth, prods. "Neil DeGrasse Tyson on Science Literacy." *Moyers & Company*. PBS. New York, NY, 10 Jan. 2014. Television.
4. This quote was originally taken from a post on the website DailyMail.com, but they have since taken down the article. I'm not sure why. John Lennox has spoken a lot on this argument though, and you can find it on various places online. I recommend his debate with Richard Dawkins or the YouTube video "Bethinking 2/6: John Lennox on Stephen Hawking's 'The Grand Design'."
5. Head, Tom, ed. (2006). *Conversations with Carl Sagan (1st ed.)*. Jackson, MS: University Press of Mississippi. ISBN 1-57806-736-7. LCCN 2005048747. OCLC 60375648.
6. Matthew 9:16-17.

Chapter 13 Hamster Prison Break

1. *Austin Powers: International Man of Mystery*. Dir. Jay Roach. By
    Mike Myers. New Line Cinema Presents, 1997. Transcript.
2. Palmeri, Tara. "Rich Manhattan Moms Hire Handicapped Tour
    Guides so Kids Can Cut Lines at Disney World." *NYPost.com*. New
    York Post, 14 May 2013. Web. 31 May 2016.
3. Hiatt, Brian. "Mumford & Sons: Rattle and Strum."
    RollingStone.com. N.p., 28 Mar. 2013. Web. 31 May 2016.
4. See 2 Corinthians 5:20.

Chapter 14 Behind Burned Doors

1. Stone, Matt, and Trey Parker. "Safe Space." *South Park*. Comedy
    Central. New York, NY, 21 Oct. 2015. Television.
2. Matthew 13:32.
3. Matthew 13:19.
4. Matthew 13:19.
5. Galatians 6:9.
6. See Hebrews 4:12.
7. See John 6:54 and Matthew 16:24.
8. Matthew 16:18.
9. See Matthew 7:5.

Chapter 15 Please Like Me

1. Daniels, Greg. "Fun Run." *The Office*. NBC. New York, NY, 27 Sept.
    2007. Television.
2. Crystal, Billy. "Grandpa." *Still Foolin' 'em: Where I've Been, Where
    I'm Going, and Where the Hell Are My Keys?* New York: Henry Holt
    and, 2013. 233. Print.
3. Lipton, James, and Billy Joel. "#6.1" *Inside the Actors Studio*. Bravo.
    New York, NY, 14 Nov. 1999. Television.
4. See Matthew 7:5.

Chapter 16 Stick of Dynamite

1. *The Great Muppet Caper.* Dir. Jim Henson. By Tom Patchett and Jay Tarses. Perf. Jim Henson, Frank Oz. Henson Associates, 1981. Transcript.
2. You may know Dan Heath and his brother Chip from their best-selling books *Made to Stick*, *Decisive* and *Switch*. This example he spoke on is also in *Switch*.
3. See Luke 10:37.
4. Matthew 7:13-14.